Feel a pr … natural horrors … world. This co … casts a dazzling light upo… …itchcraft and the occult. Read of frightening real-life encounters with apparitions, arcane magic, demons, poltergeists, and possessions.

Inside are chronicles of several notorious locations, with unrivalled levels of detail and length.

Discover the black magic mysteries of *Clapham Wood* - marvel at the supernatural phenomenon at *Dudley Castle* - and shudder with fear at the entities that stalk the corridors at *Littledean Hall*.

Also available by Peter Drake

Tales of Ghostly Horror:

Real-life Encounters with the Supernatural

Tales of Occult Horror: Real-life Encounters with the Supernatural

ISBN: 978-1-4709-1469-1

Note on cover artwork: the symbol of the pentagram was widely used in the ancient world. It has been found in Sumerian writing dating back to at least 3000 BC. The pentagram has occult and magical associations, and is now more commonly a symbol of faith for Wiccans and neopagans.

CONTENTS

PREFACE

"There are horrors beyond life's edge that we do not suspect, and once in a while man's evil prying calls them just within our range."

H.P. LOVECRAFT

This is a sequel to a book I published last year, entitled: 'Tales of Ghostly Horror: Real-life Encounters with the Supernatural.' It proved surprisingly successful, particularly in Kindle format and in the United States of America. Naturally, my thoughts turned to creating another collection of authentic paranormal stories.

'The Occult' literally means knowledge of the unknown, or the unseen, and it is a broad, generic term for supernatural phenomenon. It is a fitting description for these thirteen tales of demons, ghosts, poltergeists, possessions, and premonitions. The occult is more often a synonym for witchcraft and black magic; and these bleaker elements seem to have infiltrated much of the book.

Witchcraft is acutely present in modern society. The vast majority of white magic's acolytes (Wiccan or otherwise) are harmless; they wish to develop their own spiritual understanding, or perhaps attempt minor enchantments. However, any involvement in witchcraft will potentially attract real dangers of a physical, spiritual and psychological nature. This holds true whether or not you believe in the power of unearthly forces and the supernatural: if the 'eternal soul' is not threatened, then certainly there are risks to mental health and to preservation of one's life. It is well-advised to avoid practitioners of black magic at all costs.

I do not pretend to be an expert; hence all mistakes, factual or otherwise, are purely my responsibility.

I must emphasise that the thirteen stories are based on genuine incidents and locations. They are not fictional. I have interviewed participants or spectators of the incidents described, and refer to background material.

Acknowledgments to everyone who helped with this book, with special mentions for Charles Walker - Dave Ball – Liz Cormell – Paul Dyason – Dawn Goding – World Oneiric Life Force (WOLF) – Dr. David Riley - Sue Ellis - Sue Latham and everyone at Paranormal Hauntings Investigations (PHI) - Christine Bosworth - Alex Oldman - and Kirsty Law.

A note for readers in the United States of America and the rest of the world: all the locations discussed in this book are in England.

THE CORNISH DEMON

Interview with Dave Ball

"It's the only time that I have been seriously hurt by a ghost," said Dave Ball. "It was a clever, manipulative ghost. It set a trap for me." Dave is the co-founder of World Oneiric Life Force (WOLF), a paranormal research team.

He received an invitation to stay at his friend Mark's house in Cornwall for a couple of days. The offer was enthusiastically accepted: Dave was looking forward to a relaxing holiday by the sea, soaking up the sun and gorging on Cornish pasties. The property was set in countryside along narrow roads and sparsely dotted with neighbouring cottages. On approaching the front door Dave could see that farm animals were kept in the extensive back garden, with chickens and goats among them. It exuded a rural wholesomeness.

Mark was glad to see him, and revealed the actual reason for bringing him to the South West. He needed his help. Knowing that Dave has psychic sensitivity and experience of investigating 'bumps in the night,' Mark apologised for embroiling him in the paranormal disturbances that were terrorising his family. In this pleasant cottage resided an otherworldly presence filled with malice.

"He was walking his dog one night," said Dave, relating what his friend had told him. "He saw something like a fire burning at the edge of woods not far away from his house. It seemed strange. When he got home he went upstairs and looked through a window; he used binoculars to look across the field. He saw people around a fire, and some kind of worship was going on – there were rituals and things. Then suddenly they all stopped and looked across to his house. They knew he was watching them. He knew they could see him. He shut the curtains, because he was scared."

Nothing else happened that night, and in the morning Mark walked over to the field at the edge of the wood. He was unable to find any traces of a fire. There were no obvious signs of the worshippers or their rituals.

Some days later Mark woke early in the morning for work. He was eating his breakfast and happened to glance out of the window to the back garden. He was shell-shocked by what he saw. One of his goats was lying dead on the ground. He raced out and found that a large circular cutting had been made in its chest and the heart had been torn out. He guessed that someone had stolen into the garden during the night and silently murdered the creature before mutilating it. There was no way a fox had done this damage. There was plenty of blood on the ground, but no sign of the heart – it was missing.

There have been other recent examples of ritualistic killings of animals in the South-West of England: in early 2011, a number of goats were found cruelly slaughtered in a small farming community in Devon.[1] Their necks had been broken, and their heads twisted to face backwards. One had its throat cut open. A local farmer who lost two of his goats in this manner recognised it had something to do with the occult. It is suggestive of a person (or people) with a strong streak of sadism and blood-thirstiness, perhaps with psychopathic tendencies. There is the idea that serial killers begin their careers with the murder of animals, progressing to children and finally to adults.

This marked the beginning of a time of fear for Mark and his family. He automatically linked the murder of his goat to the worshippers from across the field, and he was frightened that they might try to get into the house. Mark was worried that people brutal and skilled enough to butcher a goat in complete silence and in darkness were a danger to his wife and children.

Mark was wrong to fear an attack from outside – because something was already in the house. The poltergeist activity did not begin slowly or imperceptibly - the outburst was impossible to miss. On one occasion, his wife had loaded the dishwasher and turned it on

---

[1] See page 41

before leaving to answer the phone; moments later she heard a huge crash in the kitchen, and ran to see what had happened. It was a picture of chaos: the trays of the dishwasher had been pulled out, with cups and dishes flung everywhere. She took photographs of the kitchen in this dreadful state, and they were shown to Dave. He said they were "unnerving, very strange," and it certainly did not look like an accident. The family also reported that flowers in a vase in the front room would be rearranged when they were not looking. "There was strong paranormal activity at the house, a strong demonic presence," said Dave.

It was too much for Mark's wife, who took herself and the children to her parents' house. This presented a perfect opportunity to tackle the uninvited presence. To this end, Dave had been invited to the house. They were joined by two of Mark's friends, to help with an investigation.

They held vigils in the downstairs lounge. It was night-time, quiet, yet with a subtly-charged atmosphere. When they moved upstairs to a bedroom they heard noises from downstairs, from the room where they had just been sitting. "It was like a metal bowl being moved against stone," said Dave. "It was grating. Everybody was unnerved, and did not want to go downstairs to check the noise. Even Mark was too scared to go down there. So I volunteered to go downstairs."

He was reluctant but felt compelled to discover what was down there. Dave knew something was there, waiting for him: "I felt that it was highly intelligent. It knew why we were there and it didn't like it."

Dave stood at the top of the steep staircase and looked down into the darkness. The noise stopped. It was silent again, with a hint of menace. There was a sense that something was about to happen. With a sudden moment of clarity Dave realised it was a ploy – 'It' had made the noise to draw a person away from the others, because it wanted them to be alone at the edge of the stairs. It was a trap.

There was a hefty push to Dave's back and he was flung down the stairs. As he was falling he grabbed hold of the rail and barely managed to keep hold. "It was all I could do to stop myself going arse over tit," he said. He was badly shook-up by the fall, but otherwise uninjured.

It was enough to convince Dave that something malevolent and dangerous was genuinely haunting the house. Mark asked if he could do anything to get rid of it: Dave explained that he had no magic solution, he was just an investigator. He advised Mark to seek the help of a priest in dissipating the evil presence. When Dave visited again, five months later, the poltergeist activity had dropped. No more animals had been killed, and the occultists had not been spotted. It was a happy ending.

WHITTINGTON CASTLE

Personal account of a paranormal investigation

Whittington Castle lies in North Shropshire, England.[2] It was a stronghold for the Saxons under King Offa in the 8th century, and was replaced with a Norman motte-and-bailey castle in the 12th century. This occurred during the tumultuous nineteen years of English history known as 'the Anarchy' – a period of incessant civil war, bloodshed and upheaval between 1135 and 1154. These early defences were probably made of wood, perhaps with walls of sharpened timber posts. The castle passed into Welsh hands several times, but always came back under English control.

The Fitzwarine family held the castle and lands from 1204 until 1420. During the 13th century there was extensive refortification, with elaboration of the moats, keeps and walls, and the use of stone materials. The 18th and 19th centuries saw an obvious decline, as much of the stone was removed for road and house building.

---

[2] http://www.whittingtoncastle.co.uk. Many thanks to Sue Ellis, castle manager at Whittington, for her help with its history.

Now the castle and grounds are managed by the local community, and have undergone significant restoration.

Among the legends associated with Whittington Castle is that of the mythical Marian Chalice, considered by some to be the actual Holy Grail. It allegedly passed into the hands of Sir Fulk Fitzwarine, lord of Whittington Castle and a 13th century descendant of the grail's time-honoured guardians. Sir Fulk kept it tucked safely away in a chapel at the castle.

There are stories of supernatural phenomenon: small ghostly children have been seen walking through walls at Whittington Castle. Unexplained noises have been heard in the tower, beneath which is a dungeon. Shadowy entities have been spotted; along with mysterious footsteps, cold spots and feelings of dread. Light anomalies have also been caught on film by ghost-hunting group Dead Haunted Nights: "One of the most compelling pieces of footage is a light that travels across a landing and appears to disappear into a wall. The shape appears to change as it moves across the screen and was only discovered when the tape was being reviewed. The group also heard stone-throwing noises as it attempted to contact spirits near an old dungeon."[3]

---

[3] http://www.shropshirestar.com/news/2010/06/07/ video-ghostly-goings-on-at-whittington-castle-shropshire/#ixzz1EATwCcfZ

Investigation

WOLF is the acronym for World Oneiric Life Force, a paranormal research team. In February 2011, they held an investigation at Whittington Castle; the team members attending were Dave Ball, Liz Cormell, Paul Dyason, Rachel Penny and Simone Taylor. Sue Ellis is the castle manager at Whittington Castle, and she monitored the events. Joining proceedings were two members of the public who had asked to join the WOLF party, and myself.

I knew nothing about Whittington Castle, as I prefer to attend these things without previous knowledge of a location's history. I cannot blame my sub-conscious for influencing anything I might experience.

The castle's authorities denied WOLF the use of Ouija boards, but they had plenty of alternative equipment to call upon: laser thermometers, static thermometers, EMF (electro-magnetic field) meters, trigger objects (including a 17th century pewter plate and mug), Dictaphones, the usual cameras – and a bell, for use in divination.

The experiment

Paul Dyason was conducting an interesting experiment. It was a variation on the stone-tape theory, where inanimate materials such as stone absorb energy and 'record' events for later replay as ghostly apparitions and events. Paul wanted to see if water at a location retained residual energies of this kind. He gathered water from the castle's moat, and into this placed a quartz crystal which he had 'cleansed,' hoping that the crystal would absorb the energy from the water and show an increased EMF reading afterwards. The initial EMF readings for the water were zero and for the quartz crystal around 1 or 1.5, its natural level.

I suggested that the water cycle ensures that the water in the moat is unlikely to be the same water which was there in the Middle Ages or even last year.

He admitted his lack of expectations: "I enjoyed this investigation, especially as I managed to get the water out of the moat for my experiment without falling in! The water experiment wasn't the most successful, unfortunately, but as I mentioned on the night, you never know what results you're gonna get - that's why they're experiments! I will try to put my thinking cap on a bit to see if this experiment can be tweaked to improve it for the future."

"It's just an experiment," he said. "Nothing ventured, nothing gained."

The tower ruins

Things began well. EMF spikes were recorded both at the tower ruins and at the cafe, and Liz Cormell (who is claircogniscent and a medium) seemed to be getting plenty of information: "There are good and bad things here. I've already got a date – oh yes, lots of activity! My cape's got the energies going!" Liz referred to a long, green cloak she was wearing. "Something's watching me!"

Simone's feelings were mixed: "I've got more from the modern things." However, the more-recent looking sections of the castle may be quite old as they have received a refurbishment that hides their age. The modern-look could be a misleading façade.

All buildings in the vicinity, such as the castle shop, cafe and offices, were kept securely locked during the investigation. This prevented interference by the public when investigating the buildings, as the castle ruins are openly-accessible. During the night I saw no wayfarers in the grounds. We were left alone.

The WOLF team seemed drawn to the huge remains of the 12th century tower. It was encircled by the old moat and reached across a bridge. The segments closest to the moat seemed mostly complete, but ruined on the other side. There was no roof, and a wooden floor covered what I believed was another level beneath.

Sue Ellis, the castle manager, later told me that this was the Inner Gatehouse tower, part of the Inner Bailey. It had a dungeon underneath, or, more precisely, an 'Oubliette' – a small chamber or chambers which were accessible only from a hatchway in a high ceiling, covered perhaps with a metal grill. There would be no light and no fresh air, and very little space in which to move. Prisoners were lowered down (or thrown down) and abandoned here in abysmal conditions. Sue said it had been "well-used" between the 12th to 15th centuries.

Standing inside the ruined tower, Simone seemed excited by a corner which had a small window shaped into a cross. She sensed something, some kind of energy. Dave Ball had been sitting with Simone. "I picked up on a young female," he said. "She had a turned up nose. She was in the keep area, she was residual."

There was table tipping over the dungeon. People stood around a small table, each placing a finger on a down-turned glass, asking spirits to move the glass and the table. Rachel Penny was asking for spirits to come forward and touch the table, to use the energy around the table. "Did it rock, then? Was it the wind?" someone asked, after the table seemed to move. Liz said she sensed something moving by her leg, and told us it was a cat. Not a real cat – a phantom cat.

Moments later she alerted the group that she had succeeded in gaining information. Liz is a medium, and can gather information such as the names and details of entities. It is "just put in my head." In this case, she came across the term, 'Gardeloo,' which is apparently similar to an old-fashioned French word for toilet, spoken as a warning when human waste was thrown from a window. Given the building's history as a dungeon, it is possible that this French word might have been frequently used in a bastardised form in this location and for the said purpose: for disposing of prisoner's faeces.

The old courtroom

After concluding the table tipping, the group moved to another part of the castle, closer to what seemed like an old gateway entrance. Earlier in the evening on a safety tour we had been ushered into a large, rectangular room used for a wedding exhibition. It was basically a function room. Tapestries adorned the high walls. People sensed something was there, and Liz had placed a pewter plate as a trigger object in the corner of the room, hoping that it would be moved by an entity.

As we walked back into the room I noticed a strong scent that had not been there previously. "It's like sweet wood smoke," sniffed Liz. It reminded me of incense, or some kind of scented firewood. "I've never smelled this here before," said Sue, who enters the room on a daily basis. When she suggested that the recent lime painting of the room might be responsible, one of the members of the public who was present – coincidentally a master mason from Lancashire – said he was certain that this was not possible.

There were cries of surprise when someone thought the trigger object have been moved. I was dubious: when I looked at the pewter plate, it did not look as if it had been moved from its original position.

We sat in a circle as the lights were turned off, making it very dark in the room. Everyone held hands, with feet touching to avoid accidental (or deliberate?) foot tapping. In the middle of the group was placed an EMF meter, set to bleep if any abnormalities were scanned. WOLF staff members called out to spirits, requesting they make themselves known, or respond to questions.

For a short while there was silence. Then there was a single tap which seemed to come from the other end of the room. Everyone heard it. I heard it. Then a moment of quiet. Then another tap, very gentle, and seeming to emanate from the same spot. Dave called out, asking if the energies in the room were making the noise and requesting that they do it again. Once again there was a moment of silence. Then – another tap.

Sue thought that it might be the underfloor heating, or perhaps the floor settling after being disturbed by people's footsteps. This is possible. But when we returned to the room later that night for another vigil, I did not hear the same taps again. Surely they would have persisted if caused by underfloor heating or the pressure from our feet.

Our efforts in the circle continued, and we encountered strange phenomenon. There were other faint footsteps and small bangs, possibly due to mundane reasons. Then Liz told us that her right ear was feeling really warm, while her other ear was very cool. I was sitting next to Liz, and her right ear felt roasting hot upon touching it, while her left ear was cool and clammy, just as she said. Paul used a laser thermometer to search for unusual heat signatures in our vicinity, but there was nothing substantially different to the rest of the room.

After a few minutes I could feel my left ear becoming very warm. I cannot explain it. The rest of my face was cool, including my nose and ear, so it could not have been a general warming-up which would have affected the rest of my face. It was a vivid heat, and a peculiar surprise.

Information was psychically-gained by Liz and Dave. Liz thought there was a male, ecclesiastic type moving around the room, looking at the group. "But it's not a chapel," she said, trying to glimpse into what previous surroundings this entity was moving. Dave sensed the presence of a boy hiding in the room, skiving off work and having a blow to his head. "Having his ears boxed?"

he mused. Then Dave, embarrassed, told us that he was getting a swear-word repeatedly spoken – "Fuck" was the word. Sue explained that he could be mistakenly identifying the name Fulk, which was the first name of the man who constructed the building, Sir Fulk Fitzwarine. She related how the name 'Fulk' was borne by all his heirs over the succeeding generations. Liz and Dave both had a sense that a debt was important to the shadowy figures they could sense in this room; they felt that land and men was owed, not money.

Sue revealed that the room's original purpose was as a courtroom, and the structure in which it reposed was the Gatehouse Tower, which dates back to the 12th century. It had served for legal purposes until the 1830s. I suggested that ownership of land and castles was an important issue during the Anarchy in the 12th century, when the castle was fortified. Perhaps this history was influencing Dave and Liz's sensations.

"It is said that there was a dungeon underneath," said Sue, later, "but this whole Gatehouse Tower was restored in 1819 and [the dungeon] was then filled in with rubble." She also informed me about the courtroom's paranormal associations: "It was also used from 1890s to after the First World War as an ironing room for the laundry. Children have been picked up in here. Also, a haughty man who dislikes people being disrespectful, [and] a woman who is scared. Also a man died in this room during the ironing phase and he is said to haunt this room. Also soldiers have been picked up from the First and Second wars."

Shock and awe

Opposite to the old courtroom are the castle shops and, above them, the offices. This was possibly a Tudor cottage, and, before that, part of the castle's Barbican and outer bailey - thus part of the castle's fortifications. The bookshop had an interesting feature: a well set in the middle of its floor, partially filled in and covered by a glass panel. Liz said she could feel energies here, both in the old well and in the books.

Across a corridor from the book shop was a gift shop. Joined to this was a smaller room - the guardroom. It was sparsely adorned, with replica-stocks, a ball-and-chain. It had a stone floor. During the initial tour of the castle I had stood by its doorway, and for no apparent reason I began to experience 'bad feelings.' I will not exaggerate what I felt, which is difficult enough for me to describe; it was like a slight tightness in my chest and head. I cannot remember ever feeling like this during a paranormal investigation before. I kept it to myself to avoid planting ideas in anyone's sub-conscious mind.

Sue Ellis had plenty of information regarding what is called the guardroom: "This was part of the barbican of the castle. A barbican was a narrow passageway leading from the Gatehouse with four towers. This was another form of defence to protect the Inner Bailey and main castle. We call it the guardroom as it makes sense that this could have been a place for soldiers to wait to go on duty. Also it could have been used for animals, weapon storage, et cetera. [There are] no stories of murders but, of course, this is likely."

I was surprised that several people felt that the upstairs section had a greater ambience. "[The castle] seemed to me to have an atmosphere about it," said Paul, "especially the upstairs landing area above the gift shop area. If I could feel it in there then it certainly must have had an [atmosphere] about it with me being probably one of the least sensitive of the group, if at all!"

Like Paul, I would never claim to have any strong psychic sensitivity, but the upstairs landing did not unsettle me; only the guardroom felt unusual. Later that night I joined a vigil in the guardroom, sitting alongside Simone, Paul, Liz and Sue. With the lights turned off it was almost pitch-black, muted illumination coming from a ceiling window.

Simone reported a disturbing sensation: she said it felt like her head had been cut in half, with pressure on her cheekbones, like they were coming apart. "This is the weirdest feeling I've ever had," she said. Liz reported the same thing, and picked up on a "battle with arms" between two brothers, the eldest sibling killed by the younger over a title. She dated it to some time in the 13th century, perhaps in the 1260s. Whittington Castle was under Welsh control between 1265 and 1282, around the date when Liz said the fight happened. She could have sensed echoes of a violent dispute from these years. Both Liz and Sue said they felt that something was in the corner, walking by them and watching them.

Simone reported feeling sick, and a few moments later I felt slightly nauseous. I did not say anything, to avoid jumping on the bandwagon. Perhaps the enclosed conditions and darkness were affecting us, or I had experienced auto-suggestion.

Everyone else now joined the vigil in the guardroom. There seemed to be more activity here than elsewhere at the castle. With my eyes now accustomed to the murky blackness I could discern what almost seemed like a shadow moving backwards and forwards, like it was pacing. I am sure that it was my eyes playing tricks on me. Others mentioned that they could see something moving in the darkness. Whether they could see something that was physically there, or saw it in a psychic sense, I was unsure.

Liz decided to sit in the doorway, where I had earlier stood and felt that strange tightness in my chest. Moments later she told us that an entity was standing right beside her, and 'it' did not like her being there. Goose pimples burst over the surface of Simone's body. Liz later described 'it' as an entity with far more awareness and intelligence that a mere echo or residual energy could possess.

Sue Ellis told us a little about the guardroom: "We have had people detect a figure who hides and pretends to be nice but is not. Also, mediums have said something about perhaps the occult in here! Children do not like this room and we only go in briefly at parties and club. The club [Fitzwarine Children's Club] takes place upstairs in the schoolroom."

We ended the vigil and moved upstairs to the offices, which are reportedly haunted. As we were waiting to move I thought I heard a footstep upstairs. Sue told me that a young boy had been seen walking through the area before, as if he were moving along a corridor that no longer existed. She believed that the offices were an area of potential paranormal activity: "It feels like someone's in there. Things happen. I haven't seen anything; but the lights can go on or off; the computer turns itself on and off."

After a short vigil in an upstairs room the group decided to move elsewhere. I was standing on the landing, next to Dave and Simone. Then we heard a door slam downstairs. It was a loud, powerful slam.

"For God's sake..!" I shouted.

Everyone was swearing and exclaiming in shock.

When I heard the door slam I immediately knew it was the guardroom door. From its direction and tenor I did not think the sound could be anything else. More momentous was the fact that everyone was upstairs. No one was downstairs, which was empty, and all the exit doors were locked. And the last person to leave the guardroom was adamant that he had left its heavy door shut.

"Come on, then, let's go and look! Come on!" cried Dave, as he, Simone and I rushed down the stairs. The rest of the group followed. It was spine-tingling stuff.

We passed through the castle shop and could see that the guardroom door was shut. There was no one in the guardroom or the shop. There was no obvious explanation for the door slamming shut. It had been left closed; and to my knowledge there were no wandering members of the public or mysterious persons downstairs to muck about. The only entrance had been locked by Sue; and in my reckoning there were no drafts or breezes that could have caused the door to slam shut so violently that I felt the building's timbers shake.

I could find no logical explanation.

Killing the atmosphere

The slamming of the door shook us up. Liz and Simone decided to stay in the guardroom by themselves, as they believed that the spirits would respond better to the presence of two females. The rest of the group moved to the offices upstairs, conducting another vigil in an area that Rachel believed was 'active.'

I noticed a sword in a scabbard on top of a bookcase (it had jabbed into my head as I stood by the bookcase, and it was damned sharp) and I suggested taking it to the guardroom for use as a trigger object – not in the traditional sense, but to trigger an outburst of activity from supernatural entities. If the creature stalking the room had been killed by such a weapon, surely it would react to the sword? Liz and Simone would be safe enough – and if not, there was our evidence for paranormal activity! I was sure that they would be willing sacrifices in the name of unearthly discovery.

Unfortunately the sword seemed to kill the atmosphere. Liz later told me that the mood had fizzled out as soon as I had entered the room with the sword (perhaps the entity had been scared away?) and nothing more happened. The mood seemed changed in the building. It was quietly dead again.

The night's investigation moved towards closure. There was a renewed vigil in the old courtroom. A bell was hung from the chandelier in hope of enticing entities into moving it in response to questions, but it did not work. That marked the end of the investigation at Whittington Castle.

Further information

http://www.wolf-rs.co.uk

(Official website for

World Oneiric Life Force)

http://www.whittingtoncastle.co.uk

(Official website for Whittington Castle)

PENDLE HILL

Interviews with Dave Ball

and Paul Dyason

The story of the Pendle witches is one of the most famous in English occult history. Pendle Hill rises high above north-east Lancashire, close to Burnley and Clitheroe. In the 17th century it was a wild and lawless place – a windswept point of rugged isolation. In 1612, twelve people from this area were put on trial for witchcraft, perversions, and murder. This so-called coven of witches had met in several cottages at Pendle Hill, ostensibly for the purpose of conducting dark rites. The public ordeal became known as the Lancashire witch trials, as they were placed alongside other witches from northern England whose alleged crimes included child murder and cannibalism. One of the 'star witnesses' was the young daughter of one of the Pendle accused, coaxed into relating tales of her mother's guilt to the court. Of the twelve Pendle witches, one died in prison and just one person was declared guilty – the remaining ten were found guilty and executed by hanging.

On Halloween 2004, a 'Most Haunted: Live' event was held at Pendle Hill. They investigated Lower Well Head Farm, Bull Hole Farm, and Tynedale Farm at Pendle Hill. It is considered one of the television programme's most terrifying episodes: "Many members of the crew collapsed, being sick, with some escorted outside. Furthermore an Ouija board was spinning out of control constantly answering to all questions, culminating in the glass flying off the table and smashing on the floor, and the table itself collapsing."[4]

Dave Ball was excited by this evidence of paranormal activity: "If this was for real, then this had to be a seriously malevolent place." In early 2008, Dave and Paul Dyason travelled to Pendle Hill on a reconnaissance trip for WOLF, their paranormal research team. Inspired by the manic supernatural activity seen in 'Most Haunted' and by the location's reputation, they wanted to see it for themselves. They trudged along muddy paths, passing through a valley to get to the famous cottages at Pendle Hill. They reached Tynedale Farm. Its barn had been converted into living quarters. Lower Well Head farm is also a private home and access for paranormal investigators is not possible.

The inhabitants of Tynedale Farm told them that the stories of witchcraft and hauntings had been blown out of proportion. Paul was suspicious of their dismissive warnings: "They told us that everything that got in 'Most Haunted' was made up; but I can't help but think that the locals are just saying this to keep the likes of us

[4] http://en.wikipedia.org/wiki/Most_Haunted_Live!#2004

away. I feel that there is an atmosphere around there that [feels] a bit tense."

"We picked up some serious stuff," said Dave. "Around the cottage was a presence which wanted us out. I phoned Simone [Taylor] on my mobile phone, whispering to her, telling her we were scared for our lives. We realised that no matter in what direction we ran we're in the middle of nowhere – we had to get out of here."

Dave and Paul backed away from Tynedale Farm. After a few steps they halted. There was movement in bushes nearby and they knew something was in there. They could hear it breathing. It was utterly dark – and Dave could not turn on his torch because it would disturb the local people. He was scared: "I took one step to speed walk away, when something white comes out in front of us. It was one of the most terrifying things I've experienced. We were certain it was something paranormal."

"The animal that jumped out on me was actually a sheep!" Paul admitted. "This affected me purely because Dave and I had just been hanging around outside Tynedale Farm late in the evening and it did seem to have an eerie atmosphere to it, although nothing tangible really happened. Anyway, it could have been psychological; but psychological or not, I was in a bit of a jumpy state when this sheep leapt out of a hedge and the darkness just ahead of us. Under the circumstances it did make my heart miss a few beats, I can tell you!"

This hunt for the supernatural on Pendle Hill became clueless. Their next stop was a museum close to Lancaster Prison – the location of the Assizes where the Pendle witches were on trial. Dave strode up to the main entrance, a huge, blue-metal set of doors at the front of the building. He knocked loudly on the doors, "bold as brass." After what seemed an inordinately long time, the shutter opened. A man in uniform peered out and gruffly asked what they wanted. Dave solicited a paranormal investigation of the premises, and received a less-than welcoming reply: "People usually want to get out of here, not get in." They had come to the prison by mistake: it was H.M.P. Lancaster, the prison which housed the Pendle witches and which is still in active service. The museum and old courtroom which Dave and Paul were after was actually round the back of the prison. Sheepishly they followed the prison guard's directions. "It's very haunted there," Dave said, covering his embarrassment.

Investigations by other paranormal teams at Pendle Hill have uncovered interesting information. Mediums have picked up the names and images of several individuals who match persons from the Lancashire witch trials. Members of film crews have been struck down by sudden bouts of illness. However, many individuals (including followers of Wicca) find Pendle Hill to be a bracing, energising location that does not feel evil or haunted. In the distant Neolithic past before the Pendle witches it was a site of pagan worship, and it is not surprising that some feel it is a spiritual place.

CLAPHAM WOOD

"I found ample evidence that Black Magic is practiced in London, and other cities, at the present day. Should any of my readers incline to a serious study of the subject, and thus come into contact with a man or woman of Power, I feel it is only right to urge them, most strongly, to refrain from being drawn into the practice of the Secret Art in any way. My own observations have led me to an absolute conviction that to do so would bring them into dangers of a very real and concrete nature."

– DENNIS WHEATLEY

Clapham Wood has an exceptionally dark history. A legendary story tells of a curse placed on Clapham, a small village in West Sussex, in 1288, after a disgruntled local man named Robert le Faulconer lost a court case for bodily harm against Adam le Gest, the local parson: "I call upon she who knows to damn this accursed village and all its meagre holdings. May the priesthood of this false God soon come to know their fate." There may be significance in this curse. Even a shallow trawl of Clapham's recent past reveals occult worship and ritual sacrifice in the wood – and four unexplained deaths, possibly murders, including the death of a retired Clapham vicar.

Black magic at Clapham Wood

Charles Walker has conducted a long and detailed investigation into the mysteries of Clapham Wood. He is the foremost expert on the black magic practiced here, describing "the desecration of graves, the sacrifice of animals and the practice of sexual perversion" as its common motifs, and maintains that the wood has been used for witchcraft by a secretive society known as the Friends of Hecate.[5]

Hecate (or Hekate) is an ancient goddess of magic. She was worshipped in Ancient Greece and Rome as early as 700 B.C. and perhaps long before that (for some people Hecate is synonymous with 'Heqat,' the Egyptian goddess of childbirth). She was depicted as having three heads – those of a dog, a serpent and a horse, sometimes alternating with the heads of a bull or a cow. Among the associations with Hecate were childbirth, nurturing the young, torches, gates and walls, doorways and crossroads, borders, and the wilderness. There were more shadowy links to dogs, magic and lunar lore. Over

---

[5] http://www.mysteriousbritain.co.uk/england/occult/black-magic-in-clapham-and-sussex.html

time, Hecate's portrayal became more overtly mystical, and she was closely linked with ghosts, curses, magic and witchcraft.

As the supreme guardian of the border between the earthly plane and the spirit world, Hecate had mastery over the spirits of the dead. Necromancers would invoke her when attempting to resurrect the dead. In the modern day, she is considered to be a goddess of witches and an important figure in neopagan belief.

The investigations of Charles Walker have led him to believe that the Friends of Hecate seek to utilise the energies at Clapham Wood through rituals and sacrifices, in order to conjure forth powerful supernatural forces and to control them for their own purposes. He alleges that influential public figures are among the members of this group.

This is reminiscent of the notorious 'Hellfire Club,' which has existed in different incarnations over the past few centuries. In the 18th century, its ranks contained politicians and magistrates, and for some time was based at the Hellfire Caves in Buckinghamshire, where it reputedly held orgies and occult rituals.[6]

---

[6] For further information on the Hellfire Caves, see Peter Drake, *Tales of Ghostly Horror: Real-life Encounters with the Supernatural*, 2010, pages 129-32

Mr. Walker began his research into Clapham Wood and the enigmatic Friends of Hecate in 1975. Media interest in a flurry of UFO sightings had dwindled, replaced by stories of dogs going missing in Clapham Wood. They would wander off during walks in the woods and were not seen again. In one case, a dog became ill after running off, returning in frenzy and foaming at the mouth, with its eyes bulging out. This followed reports of people experiencing feelings of nausea, stomach cramps and sickness while walking along footpaths in the wood or in the proximity of St. Mary's Church, situated on the edge of the woods, isolated from Clapham village.

In November 1978, Mr. Walker was contacted by a mysterious stranger who alerted him to the existence of the Friends of Hecate and their activities. The stranger was a member of this group, and described how it had formed in Sussex; it used Clapham Wood and the surrounding area for its mystical energies. They made ritualistic sacrifices, choosing anything from a wide range of domestic and farm animals - but usually a dog, to honour Hecate's close association with these creatures. In Ancient Greece and Rome, dogs were often sacrificed to Hecate and the offering left at crossroads in her honour; and since several ley lines cross at Clapham Wood, this possibly influenced the choice of location.

A macabre explanation for the disappearance of dogs might be found in necromantic rituals – the reanimation of the dead. In preparation for such an awesome feat, it was necessary for the sorcerer to consume nothing but black unleavened bread, unfermented grape juice, and dog's flesh. Eating dogs would put the sorcerer in rapport with Hecate, the goddess of death, because it is her creature. Perhaps those pets that went missing in Clapham Wood were taken for someone's meal. The best corpses to reanimate are supposedly those freshly dead, as their spirits hover closer to their bodies. Given the fact that several people were found dead after long disappearances in the 1970s and early '80s (see below), it is not inconceivable that an individual or a group with a deep obsession with the occult sought to resurrect the murder victims.

To return to Charles Walker's story, there are aspects which have caused people to question its logic. The stated intention of the stranger in 1978 who gave information to Mr. Walker was to cool his interest in the woods; but this obviously had the opposite effect. The disappearance of dogs could have a less-morbid explanation, and the Friends of Hecate might just be harmless pagans that worship in the woods at Clapham. But Mr. Walker adamantly defends the findings of his research.

Occultism in modern England

Given recent news stories and interviews for this book, it would seem that witchcraft and occult worship are still active in modern England. The gatherings of occult groups lessened in the 1980s, because of the press attention and the damage caused to Clapham Wood after the Great Storm of 1987. In the 1990s, Mr. Walker became aware of an unusual number of animals going missing again, with evidence that locations in Sussex and close to Clapham were used for occult gatherings. Mr. Walker believes the Friends of Hecate have contacts or members living in Clapham. I asked Mr. Walker for his opinions on whether occult-type activities were increasing at Clapham Wood and other areas in 2011:

> *"As far as animals going missing or being slaughtered in the Clapham Wood area - that activity has not increased at all. If anything I think the publicity may just have caused a decrease in such activity. However, having said, general occult activity in the area does not seem to have decreased at all. You will still find occasional indications of rituals in the wood, particularly near the large beech tree.* [Probably the 'Altar Tree' discussed later.]
>
> *"There is woodland opposite that large tree which many people have described as 'creepy, heavy,*

oppressive et cetera'. I have taken several mediums/psychics to that spot and most prefer to leave the area as soon as possible. Paranormal activity in the area is still very, very high and it is, I am certain, increasing.

"The increased activity in the West Country is a little disturbing, as whilst researching Clapham Wood, information came to light suggesting that the original group, The Friends of Hecate, were setting up groups in that area, as well as moving East towards Brighton, Hastings, Kent and Essex."

He alleges that black magic is practiced in many other parts of the South and South West of England, such as Dartmoor, Tintagel, Eastbourne and Arundel.

In early 2011, the Daily Mail reported the brutal slaughter of four goats in Tipton St. John, a small Devon village. They were killed within three days of each other, either with their heads twisted to face backwards or with their throats cut. Jimmy Small, a local farmer who lost two animals, said: "Everyone is talking about it and locals are keeping their eyes open. I recognise it could have something to do with the occult. One of my goats was left dead foaming at the mouth with a swollen belly. The other I found dying and crying with its head twisted backwards. This has horrified locals. What sort of people could do this?"

In December 2010, members of the West Midlands Ghost Club (WMGC) visited Hopwas Wood, which is located outside Tamworth in South Staffordshire. They had heard about a tall, ghostly figure that had been sighted there.[7] In their background research, the WMGC discovered that Hopwas Wood had once been the site of witchcraft-like activities. There were eye-witness accounts of a gathering of occultists interrupted in full-swing by police on the night of the summer solstice (21st June) in 1984; sixteen witches were seen nakedly "dancing and chanting around a fire" in a clearing, attempting to roughly form the shape of a pentagram as they conducted magical rituals. They were found in possession of food, drink, and illegal drugs; and, more interestingly, they had tools for arcane magical ceremonies such as robes, a sword, wand, pentacle and a chalice.

It bears a remarkable likeness to a scene from Dennis Wheatley's 1934 novel 'The Devil Rides Out.' In his research, Wheatley spoke to leading occultists of the day, such as Aleister Crowley (the most notorious occultist of the 20th century, Crowley alleged that he communicated with demons and entities from higher spheres of existence) the Reverend Montague Summers and Rollo Ahmed. To quote the warning from his

---

[7] http://www.westmidlandsghostclub.com/page37.htm

introduction to 'The Devil Rides Out' that heads this chapter, he had "found ample evidence that Black Magic is practiced in London, and other cities, at the present day." If that was true of 1930s England, it seems most certainly the case now. In relation to the occult ceremony at Hopwas Wood, it emerged from later reports in the 'Tamworth Herald' that the majority of participants came from the Tamworth area; a few came from the West Country; and their numbers included businessmen and local notables. They belonged to an international organisation of occultists and astrologers called the 'Order of the Silver Star.' This was founded by Aleister Crowley after he was expelled from the 'Order of the Golden Dawn,' with at least one of his chief disciples becoming a leading political figure. This association would suggest that the worshippers found capering nakedly round the fire in Hopwas Wood were very possibly interested in the darker aspects of occultism.

Back to December 2010, the members of WMGC were amazed to discover a large copper plate buried beneath thick snow and a layer of earth. They used a metal detector to sweep a specific patch of land at Hopwas Wood that had exhibited signs of burning, suggesting a fire had blazed here recently. The copper plate was decorated with strange shapes and runes, possibly Enochian – a language utilised by Aleister

Crowley in his reputed communications with entities from outside our realm.

The story of Adam

One of the most highly publicised forms of witchcraft in England is Voodoo, practiced by a small number of African immigrants. It has been described as big business in cities such as London, and has been shielded from public scrutiny by a wall of silence from the immigrant community.

The story of Adam, or 'the torso in the Thames,' is a disturbing example of human sacrifice. "Adam" is the name given to a young African boy whose torso was discovered floating in the River Thames, London, on Friday, 21 September 2001. His murder is believed to be linked to a ritual killing.

According to Wikipedia:

"A passer-by crossing the bridge had noticed an orange object in the water, and realising it was a body as it passed under the bridge, alerted the police. The Metropolitan Police sent its marine search unit to the scene, who recovered the torso further downstream. The body was found to be the torso of a young black child, the orange being a pair of shorts around the stumps of the legs.

"Police soon realized after recovering only the torso, that the circumstances were unusual and not typical of a sex-related murder. It was initially suspected that the murder was a medicine murder. This type of killing involves the removal of body parts such as the ears or genitals. However Adam's genitals were not removed, and the police ruled out this theory.

"A post-mortem was carried out on Adam's remains. This established from the amount of British food in Adam's stomach and pollen in his lungs that he had only been in the United Kingdom for a few days. A potion that contained ingredients used in African ritual magic was also discovered in his stomach."[8]

The post-mortem results were grim: extracts of a West African poison found in the child's intestine were a paralysing agent, not an anaesthetic, so there is every chance he would have been conscious when murdered. He would have been unable to move or to speak. The body was found without its legs, arms and head, and had been completely drained of blood, presumably from the throat after it had been cut. The limbs and head had been removed with skilful precision. Flecks of gold were found in the intestine. These were likely added to the

[8] http://en.wikipedia.org/wiki/Adam_(murder_victim)

boy's diet to make his sacrifice and the draining of his blood more powerful.

A child's ritualistic slaughter is considered the most empowering form of human sacrifice. This idea is common to African Voodoo beliefs and Western European occultism. Dismembered body parts (usually eyes, ears and genitals) are used in medicine, for charms and potions. There is cannibalism. In the case of Adam, obtaining his blood was the purpose of his murder. Blood has been considered one of the most potent aids to magical rituals for thousands of years, across different continents and cultures.

In 2011, the identity of the boy was discovered: his name was Ikpomwosa, and he was six years old at the time of his death.[9] A woman named Joyce Osiagede was tracked to Germany, and she stated that she cared for him after his parents were deported to Nigeria. She handed the boy over to a man named Bawa, who took him to London. Despite the use of forensic science and extensive investigations, the Metropolitan Police Service has not yet caught the killer.

The sacrifice of a child in this manner is utterly disgusting and an act of terrifying depravity. It belongs in

---

[9] http://www.dailymail.co.uk/news/article-1375024/Voodoo-human-sacrifice-The-haunting-story-Adam-Torso-Thames-boy-finally-identified.html

the Stone Age, not in the so-called civilised, modern world. Whether or not you believe in ghosts, demons and the supernatural, it is difficult to dismiss the conclusion that evil lies in the hearts of men, not devils.

WOLF at Clapham Woods

Dave Ball accepts the stories of witchcraft at Clapham Wood: "In the woods, people conjure and use supernatural techniques. The place is notorious for devil worshippers, the Friends of Hecate. This is documented fact. Someone told me that once a horse went missing in the wood. A bloke was riding through there and had to answer a call of nature. He left his horse tethered, and when he came back to the path it had gone."

In 2008, Dave travelled to West Sussex to see this den of devilry for himself. Accompanying him in the pursuit of occultism was Paul Dyason. "It seemed to have an atmosphere about it," Paul said. "It almost seemed to be initially noticeable in the village, before entering the woods, where we parked. Although this could have been more of a case of having read quite a bit about this area and the woods, and the links of the village to the alleged activities in the woods playing on my mind. Once in the woods the atmosphere seemed even stronger."

As they walked along a path heading into the woods, they were unsettled by an old man hoeing his garden, who stopped to stare silently at them. The locals had already tried to dissuade them from entering the wood, issuing warnings to beware for their safety. Dave and Paul came across signs put up to deter ramblers – advising them to keep out. Whereas, in fact, there is public access. "They don't want you to see what's going on," said Dave.

Paul was impressed by the way that Clapham Wood's trees and vegetation had seemingly been shaped and designed to an inexplicable purpose:

> *"There seemed to be small branches and sticks of differing sizes that appeared to be suspended at various levels from the ground, from about waist to head height. These were snapped off and were being kept at their level by being stuck in trees and bushes. But they didn't seem to be sticks or branches that would have naturally fallen and ended up where they were. I guess there was always the chance that [they] had fallen, caught in the trees on their way to the ground, but given how many we found I think it was an unusually high amount for the area in question. Also, some of the sticks didn't seem to belong to the tree or bush that they were in, suggesting they did not fall from them. I wondered if they were deliberately put there to act as markers to show the people* [who]

put them there if anyone else has passed through the area, as they would have fallen to the ground."

This could be 'tree hexing,' where bushes and the branches of small trees are bowed and bonded (tied) together. It can occur naturally, but not to the extent seen at Clapham Wood. Charles Walker has described one area in the wood where the bonding created an area shaped into the outline of a five-pointed star. It is unlikely that will have been a natural formation.

UFOs at Clapham Wood

As they traversed deeper into the woodland, Paul noted that it seemed devoid of wildlife. There was no birdsong. Many other accounts of Clapham Wood have mentioned this absence of sight or sound of animals and birds.

Radioactive contamination could be a reason why wildlife keeps away. Examination with Geiger counters has uncovered higher levels of radiation than expected in an area with such a high chalk content, which should create below average levels. Maybe it has something to do with the large craters or depressions seen in early photographs of the landscape, taken when it was sparsely-forested. They may have been created by the impact of large meteor strikes now hidden by trees and vegetation, which has left a legacy of radioactivity.

Some have speculated that UFOs and aliens are responsible for the mysteries at Clapham Wood. Enthusiasts believe that certain regions, often small in size, are gateways for strange phenomenon. Sightings of UFOs, supernatural activity and occult worship can be found in the same specific area.

There is sighting from the 1700s of a "bright round shape like the full Moon" which floated down into the woods and disappeared, before a smell of burning material was noticed. UFOs were sighted over the woodland on several occasions in the 1960s, with reports of strange lights in the sky and aircraft landing in the wood. These sightings persisted into the 1970s and 1980s. The stories of UFOs are eerily similar to supposed landings of UFOs in Soviet-era Russia, where craft of bizarre design and propulsion were observed landing in isolated woodland, flattening trees and causing fires before leaving. These areas afterwards exhibited a higher-than usual level of radiation, and a lack of animal-life and birds.

The Altar Tree

Traversing the woodland paths at Clapham Wood, Dave and Paul emerged into a strange clearing with a central, powerful feature.

"We came across a humungous tree," Dave said, "it was huge." His photographic and video evidence show a large, exceptionally gnarled tree, dominating the clearing as its thick branches stretch into the woodland canopy. It has a wide trunk, marked by large hollows, swellings and indentations that give the impression of bodies and faces. Dave agreed with Paul's comparison to the cursed tree in the film, 'Sleepy Hollow.'

"There were remains of a big fire at the base of the tree," Dave said. "We saw runes and symbols nearby." There have been discoveries of tree stumps marked with intricately carved pentagrams in certain parts of the woods.

"There were logs on which lots of pieces of stone flint had been left," he continued. "Everything seemed to have its place, put in a certain way according to a plan. Paul found a large piece of flint in the tree which was shaped like a tool of some sort. Moments after we started looking at the tree the heavens opened and it started raining. This was torrential; this was proper rain. We thought we could hear squealing, squawking noises in the rain."

Paul believed that the clearing was likely to attract people to hang-out, perhaps teenagers, given his discovery of empty beer bottles and a waterproof sheet. "There isn't anything particularly unusual in that," he said, "but the large flint stone we found in one of the nooks and crannies of the trees roots...This flint looked like it had one end of it sharpened into a blade, and the natural shape of the stone gave itself to having a natural hand-hold, as if it was almost shaped around the hand. Given the stories regarding Hecate and sacrifices, this was particularly interesting."

They found the atmosphere to be disturbing and unnaturally quiet, but encountered no overt devil worship or paranormal activity. Dave and Paul observed tree-hexing in the 'Altar Tree' clearing, with branches, twigs and vegetation in the outlying woodland strangely bowed, stretched and arranged.

Dave and Paul's clearing is likely to have been the location for an occult ceremony. Charles Walker has mentioned how ramblers can innocently stumble across the sites of meetings, discovering the remnants of fires, candle wax, circles constructed of flint, and the remains of animals – while finding that the branches of small trees and bushes are bowed or bonded together. The clearings in the wood sometimes contain rubble from ruined buildings, possibly from medieval cottages abandoned after the local population was ravaged by the Black Death and plague in the 14th century. Rumours of plague pits filled with the dead accentuate this gruesome history, making it even more attractive as a location for occult gatherings.

A strange and bloody history

Ghosts have allegedly haunted Clapham Wood for hundreds of years. Much of it is ancient woodland, and time-honoured lore ascribes stories of apparitions, strange voices, and people being inexplicably pushed by invisible entities. There is even an account by two walkers of a strange mist forming into the shape of a large bear. In recent decades people have reported feelings of nausea and sickness after walking through the wood, and the sensation of being stalked by unseen forces.

An account was submitted to Hampshire Ghost Club from four people who, in 2008, hoped to snatch a few thrilling frights in the famous wood.[10] They arrived close to midnight. It was very dark. When in the vicinity of the local church they began hearing strange noises, and had a feeling that something was following them. Fear began to tickle their innards. They continued along the footpath. Passing murky fields, the small group could see tiny bright lights in the bushes. They did not know what they were. Then black figures emerged and began running all around them. A young woman in the group felt dizzy and collapsed, suffering from what looked like a seizure. Her eyes were rolling and her eyelids

---

[10]http://www.hampshireghostclub.net/modules/news/article.php?storyid=448

flickering. She was carried as they began to panic. The woman's friends helped to hold her up as they frantically escaped to their car. As the last person clambered over a sty, he felt something touching him and he screamed at everyone to run. Upon reaching the car they could see that the young man was very pale and had been hit in the face.

Quite possibly they had interrupted an occult gathering. This would explain the sense of being watched, the lights in the distance and black figures rushing at the unsuspecting visitors. This same group of people has visited the wood on previous occasions, and during vigils at the Altar Tree they have experienced strange lights and noises.

Other individuals who have visited Clapham Wood in 2011 report that stones are thrown by people hiding in the trees, and traps are set along the paths at night-time to cause maximum injuries.

More disturbing in the annals of Clapham's history are the four deaths that took place in the area between 1972 and 1981. Only one death was confirmed as murder, as the other corpses were discovered in too highly an advanced state of decomposition to make autopsy possible. The victims disappeared while hiking in Clapham Wood or nearby countryside; their corpses discovered anything from a few weeks to three years after they went missing. They were:

Peter Goldsmith, a policeman and former Royal Marine Commando, who disappeared across the Downs in 1972; his body was found six months later hidden in a patch of thick bramble.

Leon Foster, a pensioner, who went missing in 1975; his corpse was uncovered three weeks later by a couple searching for a missing horse.

Reverend Neil Snelling, the retired vicar of Clapham Parish. His church of St. Mary is located on the edge of Clapham Wood. On 31st October 1978 – Halloween – he visited the dentist in a nearby village and, unable to get a lift home from his wife (their car had mysteriously broken down), he told her over the telephone that he would walk home from his current position in Findon to their property in Steyning. It was a distance of only five miles, directly across Down countryside. Somewhere on that walk he went missing. Over the next few days the region was meticulously combed by police with tracker dogs, with the assistance of aircraft. There was no sign of the vicar. It was three years until his remains were found in Wiston, several miles north of the villages of Findon and Steyning. A Canadian tourist came across the body but, sickeningly, he waited until leaving the country before informing the police.

Jillian Matthews, a 37-year old divorcee with a history of mental illness. She went missing in September 1981, three weeks after Rev. Snelling's body was discovered. She was found three weeks later in a state of partial undress, having been raped and strangled to death. No one was ever found guilty of her murder.

Many have assumed a connection exists between the occult activity at Clapham Wood and these four unexplained deaths. A possible link to black magic and necromancy was discussed earlier.

Charles Walker argues there is a direct link to the Friends of Hecate:

> *"No one was brought to trial for any of the deaths associated with the Clapham case at all. From investigations myself and others conducted there, [it] seemed to be enough to assume that at least some of the deaths had a connection with occult activity. I should make it clear that witchcraft was not the cause. Dark occult activities - if we have to give it a name, the Black Magic, but not witchcraft - was involved. We were told that the main group using the area, the Friends of Hecate, would stop at nothing to protect their activities and members, and therefore perhaps the deaths were to do with that. Many have found it difficult to even consider this as a possibility but I can only relate our findings after extensive investigation. I think that it was the animals used during rituals rather than the humans. It would seem that they were just unfortunate enough to be in the wrong way or, it*

was suggested for the Reverend, discovered more than was good for them or safe for the [Hecate] group and their activities."

It is exceptionally coincidental that four people could go missing all within the same geographic vicinity, with discovery of three of the corpses occurring so long afterwards. It is highly peculiar that no one was ever charged with the murders. This left a hardened, cold-blooded killer on the loose near Clapham Wood in the 1970s and 1980s, and possibly that killer is still there.

When Dave and Paul travelled through Clapham Wood, they were entering a place that holds genuine threats to life. No wonder the locals seek to dissuade outsiders from treading its paths.

Further information

http://en.wikipedia.org/wiki/Clapham_Wood_Mystery
(An overview of the mystery)

http://www.mysteriousbritain.co.uk/england/occult/black-magic-in-clapham-and-sussex.html
(An article by Charles Walker, highly recommended for further reading)

http://www.ufodigest.com/shadowmag/occult/walker.html
(Interview with Charles Walker)

http://occultandparanormal.webs.com
(Worthing Occult and Paranormal Investigations)

http://www.freewebs.com/faeden/claphamwoodoccult.htm
(A sceptical view of Charles Walker's investigation)

http://www.findonvillage.com/0589_phone_call_from_findon.htm
(An account of the disappearance of Reverend Neil Snelling)

http://www.westmidlandsghostclub.com/page37.htm
(An account of witchcraft in Hopwas Wood, Tamworth)

SHERLOCK AT THE DOLPHIN HOTEL

Interview with Dave Ball

After completing a thought-provoking search of Clapham Wood, Dave Ball and Paul Dyason returned to Littlehampton, in West Sussex. They were staying at the Dolphin Hotel – an old coaching inn that dates back to 1735. It is reputedly haunted: the apparitions of women and children have been spotted and their ghostly voices heard. The psychic, Derek Acorah, of 'Most Haunted' fame, has declared that the hotel has many spirits.

As night fell they were joined by two resident paranormal investigators, presumably Littlehampton Investigative Ghost Hunting Team (LIGHT), as they searched for unearthly activity. Dave sensed that something was wrong:

> *"Things here didn't add up. The one room was remarkable. We were calling out to spirits when we heard tapping. To me and Paul it sounded like it was coming from the floor, but the other two were looking up: they insisted it was coming from the ceiling. I asked what was underneath the room, to discount people cheating, and they said it was a*

locked storage room; there was no space in there for a person. The tapping happened for about five minutes and was very loud, definite, borderline poltergeist activity.

"The two investigators (it was a man and a woman, a couple), they were interested in explaining what was happening. Paul took it in, but I was suspicious – the couple were busy texting all the time. When they went out, I went back in and the tapping had stopped. It'd seemed related to the text messages they were sending.

"In a corner of another room there was a doll sitting in a high chair; the bloke went to the doll and was messing with the back of it. It was furtive. Later there were orbs in the room, and I wondered if he had set something up. The cellar was supposed to be active and we wanted to go down there earlier than we were supposed to. We weren't waiting to be led any more by the couple. Then the couple had to disappear, they said they had to leave unexpectedly as their kid was being babysat and was having fits and convulsions. But later I saw them talking outside, rolling a fag with friends. They were hardly in a rush to leave as they had said.

"I rushed upstairs [in the building] *and went to the room opposite the one with tapping – the building*

was in a rough 'U' shape. I threw bits of stone at the windows of the room below this 'haunted' one, the storage room where I thought I had heard the tapping coming from; and I saw the light come on. It had sort of frosted glass, and I could see through it - I saw a sink, and a person, and I could see that it was not a storage room filled with things; it was just a normal room.

"It was all a lie, all a ruse to get paranormal groups to hire the upstairs and to actually pay to sit in darkness. The place was really unappealing and they needed business."

A veritable Sherlock Holmes, Dave proceeded to explain to Paul the unscrupulousness of how they had been duped by the Dolphin Inn. Paul had believed that all the taps and bangs were genuine supernatural phenomena, and was downhearted to learn the actual cause. He was not a happy Watson.

COALHOUSE FORT

Account of a paranormal investigation

Coalhouse Fort is a Victorian coastal defence fort. It was constructed at the Thames estuary in Tilbury, Essex to defend the approaches to London from a perceived threat of invasion from Continental Europe, and it was completed in 1874. The site has a long history due to its strategic importance: it served as a position for gun batteries during the long wars with France in the 18th and early 19th centuries; as a fort for King Henry VIII in the 16th century; and, in ancient times, as a Roman garrison camp. Coalhouse Fort retained its role as a military bastion during the First World War and the Second World War, when it was modified to allow more modern armaments, such as long-range artillery.

The complexity of Coalhouse Fort deserves a more technical description:

> *"The final design that can be seen today consists of an arc of granite-faced gun casemates with iron shields and an open battery at the up-river end. The rear of the fort consists of barracks. The magazines are on the basement level, directly beneath the guns they served. Two ditches, the inner one defended by caponiers, would have allowed the troops to defend the fort very*

effectively had it ever fallen under direct attack. The barracks themselves had bullet-proof shutters across the windows; loopholes pierced into these shutters allowed the troops to use small arms fire from the barracks against an attacking army."[11]

The fort was neglected in the post-war years but saved from terminal decay in 1983, after being leased to a voluntary organisation. Much of it was restored to near-original condition. It is now open to the public at certain times of the year.

"It's a cross between Lord of the Rings and Auschwitz," said Dave Ball. "It's a huge place. Part of it's derelict. A peculiar place. It's a haunted place!" Looking at photographs of Coalhouse Fort it seems much like a castle, with its long walls and window-like openings.

Attack of the man-wolf

Coalhouse Fort is built on marshland, and just outside its grounds is a recreation area – large and flat, perhaps a floodplain. It felt threatening to many of the WOLF team members when they arrived for a paranormal investigation. The team included Dave Ball, Liz Cormell, Paul Dyason, and Simone Taylor. They said there was a sense of "vastness and darkness." The

---

[11]http://www.undergroundkent.co.uk/coalhouse_fort.htm

females of the team were very reluctant to go to the outdoor toilets by themselves. They had seen an object darting across the plain at a high speed, perhaps an animal, and were unnerved to think that something was out there.

They were told a harrowing story by Kieron Saville, a guide at Coalhouse Fort who was taking care of them. "There was another group of investigators here outside with Kieron one or two years prior," said Dave, recalling the tale. "They heard howling on the plain, and the girls froze with fear. They saw something human-shaped, yet animal like. They saw it walking at first on two legs, then it came running towards them, falling down to all fours and suddenly running like a dog – running at vast speed. It came to a railing, stopped and leaped over it; this was five or six feet from a standing position. It landed on its feet, then looked up to the sky and howled. It was one of the most terrifying things Kieron had ever seen."

"There's something evil down here"

WOLF explored the labyrinth of passages and chambers which lie within the walls of Coalhouse Fort. Among the spirits that Dave sensed was a man who had experienced bullying: "He had been attacked, raped and murdered. We later found out it was true, that this had happened to someone there in the past." They passed through the museum area, where Kieron had told them there was an engine part to which the spirit of a pilot was attached; other paranormal groups had seen and heard him.

Simone Taylor felt uneasy at the Fort: "There's something evil down here," she said. They held a vigil in the shell rooms. There was a narrow tunnel with the rooms branching off from the sides: it was like a horse-shoe, it curved around and met another tunnel running parallel. It was pitch-black: they could not see their hands, and because of its tightness and narrowness the tunnel was very claustrophobic. The walls would have been extremely thick, making the atmosphere so much more oppressive and heavy. "A few spirits were haunting the tunnel and the rooms from the time of its use for the military," said Dave. "Before it became a museum it was a ruin, abandoned, so it was a perfect den for witchcraft and the occult. We knew of devil worship from symbols down there [carved] on the walls." There have been allegations that occult ceremonies took place in Coalhouse Fort in the 1980s, before its restoration, and left a terrible legacy of dark, malevolent energy.

The tunnel was so narrow that the WOLF team was forced to stand in a line and hold hands, barring any person from walking past. There was no one else down there. They could see an EMF meter, which would light-up and flash from green to red if there were any changes in the electro-magnetic field, indicating ghostly activity.

There were sudden knocks from the other side of the tunnel that ran parallel. Dave went by himself to investigate but could not see any one. After he returned to the group they were abruptly hit by a malign atmosphere. Dave could feel they were suddenly threatened:

> *"We were in the presence of something. There was an awful uneasiness. We were blocked; I had gone from one bad area to another. Everyone was holding hands when we heard an almighty growl. In the pitch-black the noise seemed to bounce off the walls. Liz leapt up screaming – "Go, go, go!" She pulled Simone and everyone with her. Everyone was forced out of the tunnel as it was so narrow, we had to go. We rushed out. Liz said she was not going back in there! There was no way she was going back into the tunnel! But there was me, Simone and Paul, we were, "Bloody hell, yes! We go back in!" When we did go back into the tunnel the atmosphere had gone flat."*

Paul Dyason confirmed the details of this frightening incident: "I heard the growl. We were all standing in a single-file line in the dark along one of the corridors. I was at the end next to Liz when we both heard a growl. It sounded like a stomach rumble and I looked at Liz, assuming it was her, and she looked at me thinking the same about me! When we realised that it was neither of us we then realised that we had just heard this growl come from between us."

Investigations by paranormal groups have uncovered activity that cannot easily be explained. There has been poltergeist activity, such as high-velocity throwing of stones in response to questions; a session of table-tipping culminating with the table jumping and moving by itself despite no one standing near it; and apparitions of soldiers. Dark figures have walked up to observers and disappeared. People have been lightly touched, and one person felt their neck being kissed. There are weird noises in the tunnels, such as growling and moaning, and the sound of something being dragged.

Liz picked up plenty of activity: "It was mainly marching – unsurprisingly - on the parade square in the middle of the fort. Corner of the eye stuff, but definite movement. Oh, and I also picked up a soldier being beaten very severely in the toilets which was all verified by the man who showed us round. I'd love to go back and conquer my fear of those tunnels to see what else I can pick up."

Television comes to the Fort

Coalhouse Fort was recently the location for the television series 'Ghosthunting, with The Only Way is Essex,' which screened in 2011. Yvette Fielding, star of

'Most Haunted,' was joined by several cast members from the reality T.V. series 'The Only Way is Essex.' There was mass hysteria and over-reaction from the celebrity guests during the investigation. The females had their hair pulled by invisible hands, and their legs touched; stones were thrown, though it is difficult to assess if they had fallen from windows or from the ceiling; and equally hard to gauge whether chairs which had apparently been thrown by spirits had, in fact, fallen on their own volition or been knocked over by cast or crew. The way in which the group ran from the haunted washroom after a light bulb fell and hit a person does not reflect well – why run from exactly the thing you are looking for? Nevertheless, it marks an interesting episode in the Fort's paranormal history.

Aftermath of EMF experiments

There is an aspect of Coalhouse Fort's service in the Second World War that might be pertinent. Fluctuations in electro-magnetic fields (EMF) are regarded as a key indicator of ghostly activity. Fluctuations in the electro-magnetic field can spark meters into crazy fits. Hence, EMF meters are designed to track any such changes in EMF fields. The scientific importance of electro-magnetism is familiar to anyone who knows of the groundbreaking work of Nikola Tesla (1856-1943) and his revolutionary experiments,[12] and the conspiracy theories regarding the 'Philadelphia Experiment.'[13]

During the war, Coalhouse Fort was equipped with instruments to monitor the magnetic field of ships as they left nearby docks. This was to check the effectiveness of 'degaussing,' a process in which the magnetic field of a steel-hulled ship was neutralised by fitting electrical cables around the hull and passing an electric current through them. This prevented magnetic mines from being attracted to the ship's hull. This degaussing process would have affected a very wide area: cables laid on the Thames river bed could measure the magnetic fields of passing ships and adjust the ship's equipment, if necessary. This work was considered top secret.[14]

The so-called 'Philadelphia Experiment' in 1943 has been refuted by authorities over the years as a hoax. There has been no independent verification that has satisfied sceptics. Most accounts agree that the experiment was an attempt to utilise electro-magnetism in rendering a large naval vessel invisible to sight and to

---

[12] http://en.wikipedia.org/wiki/Nikola_Tesla

[13]http://en.wikipedia.org/wiki/Philadelphia_experiment

[14] For further information:
http://en.wikipedia.org/wiki/Coalhouse_Fort

radar. As seen in the 'degaussing' work at Coalhouse Fort, electric currents were already being used to demagnetise a ship's steel hull, and it could have been another attempt to exploit the forces of nature for military purposes.

During the experiments at Philadelphia dockyards in 1943, the U.S.S. Eldridge was successfully made invisible, with a greenish fog taking its place. After its re-appearance, crew members experienced severe nausea and sickness; some sailors were embedded in the metal walls and structures of the ship, with one person having fallen through the deck – in fact passing *through* the metal deck - and finding his hand embedded and stuck in the steel hull. A subsequent experiment caused the ship to allegedly vanish and teleport to Norfolk, Virginia – over 200 miles away – sitting there for some time before suddenly vanishing again, travelling back in time for the duration of ten seconds before reappearing back in Philadelphia. The side-effects were serious for the crew: some were physically fused to bulkheads, while others developed mental illness or simply vanished without a trace.

This is not to suggest that anything similar happened at Coalhouse Fort. It is intriguing to speculate about the heavy use of electro-magnetic currents at this location. Could the Fort have been somehow charged by the proximity of this energy-field? Does it adversely affect

EMF meters? Has it empowered the supernatural forces at Coalhouse Fort?

That is another story!

DUDLEY CASTLE

Chronicle of a paranormal landmark

Dudley Castle is famous for its ghosts. For the sheer number of supernatural entities that dwell here it is jointly-ranked as the 4th-most haunted castle in the United Kingdom. According to their statistics, around 400 ghosts and 100 spirits have been spotted at the ancient castle and its world-famed zoological gardens.

There is an extensive gallery of ghoulish inhabitants:

The *Grey Lady*, said to be the spirit of Dorothy Beaumont, wife of a senior Royalist officer when the castle was besieged by Parliamentarians in 1646. She died in childbirth in the keep. There have been several sightings of her in the main grounds, and in the old chapel grieving for her lost child. She has been spotted at the rear drawbridge; in the manor ruins; outside the Queen Mary Ballroom; walking up the steps towards the keep; and walking along the keep's battlements. In 1966, a teenager working at the Zoo reported hearing "weird noises" which were accompanied by the "shape of a woman in a white gown".[15]

---

[15] http://www.dudleycastle.org.uk/miscellaneous.html

The spirit of *John de Somery*, a famously bad 'robber-lord' of Dudley Castle in the early 14th century. He was accused of committing murder and robbery to finance construction at the castle, so it is unlikely he was mourned after his death in 1321. The Undercroft contains two large stone sarcophaguses, now empty and lidless, and one of these is rumoured to have housed his remains. During the 'Most Haunted: Live' paranormal event at Dudley Castle in 2002, the medium/psychic Derek Acorah picked up on the name John Somerby in connection to one of the sarcophagus.

The *Black Monk*, an entity that has been linked to black magic. Often seen in the form of a shadowy, hooded figure. The figure of a monk has been seen looking out at the courtyard from a window in the 14th century chapel, which is directly above the Undercroft building. WOLF, a paranormal research team, reported a recent sighting of a black hooded figure walking along the top of the castle ruins.[16] During the 'Most Haunted: Live' investigation, Derek Acorah made contact with the energy of a hooded man who was attempting to conceal himself; he reappeared later that night, and was identified as a monk called Hal, who was a "devious" character. Some of the stone used to build the castle was taken from the Priory of St. James, which was

---

[16] See www.wolf-rs.co.uk

administered by Cluniac monks, an offshoot of the Benedictine Order. These monks would have worn black habits with hoods, leading some to refer to the 'Stone Tape theory' and suggest that the Black Monk is a replay of past events – as stone can supposedly absorb the emotional energy of living beings, and playback the image or sound of that person or event as a sort of recording.

The *ghosts of a young girl and a female servant*, who is a mother figure to this girl. They have been encountered at the Discovery Centre education facility, which was originally the Moat Café.

A *poltergeist*, in the Visitor Centre's former gift shop. The room is now empty, and simply acts as an exit route. According to WOLF, this shop has perhaps the highest level of activity at Dudley Castle and they believe a poltergeist is present: "A heavy shop stand was pushed over and objects have been observed falling off shelves, or being thrown across the room."[17] It featured in the 'Most Haunted: Live' event, with strange EMF meter readings taken, and Derek Acorah became aware of the presence of a spirit of a small lady, said to be responsible for the activity here. However, a WOLF investigation of the gift shop failed to uncover evidence to support this assertion. Dr. David Riley, the chief presenter at the

---

[17] ibid

castle and zoo, believes its strange activity has moved next door: "To be honest we don't [have] much activity in the gift shop now, it is more centred around the chequer board room." This latter room is adjacent to the old gift shop.

A *drummer boy*, who haunts the outer gateway. He is said to have served in the English Civil War (1642-51) during which time the castle was sorely besieged by Parliamentarian forces. He was shot in cold blood and bled to death in the outer gateway that is now referred to as the Drummer-boy gate. This is a large, solid structure, with a steep path leading down through the now-empty archway, the gates having long-since disappeared. An apparition of the drummer boy has been sighted and his eerie drumming heard. He is considered a particularly bad omen for those who encounter him.

The ghost of *Sir John Dudley*, Duke of Northumberland. He was the right-hand man of King Henry VIII and protector of King Edward VI; but after a failed attempt to place his daughter-in-law, Lady Jane Grey, on the throne of England in 1553, he was executed for treason by Queen Mary. His ghost is alleged to haunt the castle which was once his home. Some critics point out that Sir John Dudley probably spent more time in London than in the castle.

A *phantom bear*. For years, there were local rumours that a tecton-style enclosure named the 'Bear Ravine' was haunted by the apparition and melancholy cries of a bear. "You don't see the bear, but you can sense it," said Chrissy, a team member from Paranormal Hauntings Investigations (PHI). She smiled enigmatically: "It's not always on all fours, it's on two legs." There was also a sighting near the enclosure of a ghostly man and woman dressed in 1930s attire and holding hands. There is a story that when excavating for the building of the tecton enclosure in the 1930s, a fifteen-metre deep crevice was unexpectedly uncovered, and, more gruesomely, a woman's skeleton was discovered. The bear ravine has been empty for years; the enclosure is crumbling and overgrown with vegetation. No unusual activity has been reported here in recent years.

Haunted tunnels. Subterranean canals link the limestone cavern system which exists beneath this geologically-rich part of Dudley. A miner has been listed among the castle's ghosts.

White Legs. There have been several reports of ghostly 'white legs.' They have been seen in the sarcophagus in the Undercroft, which is an old crypt. An employee in the Visitor Centre saw something similar and people at the PHI vigil in the Undercroft reported seeing a pair of white legs, as detailed later.

'Olde-worlde' apparitions. In the 1930s, a guide was giving two visitors a tour of the castle when they all witnessed a bizarre sight, close to the triple gateway. As recollected by the guide: "It happened on a fairly quiet afternoon. I was sitting at the bottom of the castle keep with two other people, in full view of the doorway, when suddenly two elderly people came around from the keep dressed in either 17th or 18th century clothes. They were walking arm-in-arm and the man held a crooked walking stick and wore a very tall hat. They walked straight past us and up into the keep. I went up after them, but there was no-one there - they had just disappeared."

The haunted cottage

A location worthy of special attention is a crumbling, derelict cottage, known as 'Harry Hatch's Cottage,' after an ex-zookeeper. It is a particularly active spot in the castle grounds. Its neighbour is the outer gatehouse, with its drummer-boy ghost.

There are tales of murder and bloodshed at the cottage. A tragic story tells how a father killed his unmarried daughter in the cottage after discovering that she had become pregnant outside of marriage. Their spirits allegedly haunt the cottage - the father's face has been seen staring through the window; and the daughter was spotted inside the cottage, rocking herself with her hands clasped around her knees.

In Victorian times the cottage was the scene of another act of bloodshed, after a man murdered his wife and two young children in the dwelling. Many people believe they have sighted this man's apparition; and EVP (electronic voice phenomenon) evidence has caught the voices of children and an angry unidentified male.

The cottage was originally part of the wall connecting the outer gate to a gatehouse at the corner. It integrates some of the original stonework and runs along the same line of trajectory. The cottage is ivy-covered and quaint; a cursory glance suggests that it is in decent condition, and many visitors to the castle say they would like to live here. But it is suffering a prolonged collapse. There are huge wooden supports at the rear of the property which prevents it sliding down a steep bank, and there is a dangerous hole at the end of the cottage pathway, part of a collapsed tunnel that once connected the corner gatehouse to the large 'drummer boy' gateway. It is now closed off to the public after being condemned as a safety risk. "There's no money to sort it out," said Dr. David Riley. "It would cost millions. The National Lottery aren't interested. So it will just be allowed to collapse."

For some, the cottage has a nasty, unnerving atmosphere. Chrissy, from PHI, had a vivid psychic experience at the cottage: "It was like a horror film.

Suddenly they were there; I saw them - a man, a woman and a child. The child had plaits in her long hair, and I had the feeling that she and her family were Austrian. I could smell German sausages. I sensed that this whole family were killed by the man."

It seems illogical that Austrians would be living at Dudley Castle, but it is worth remembering that the site has a long history stretching back to 1071 and perhaps much earlier than that. It is conceivable that Saxons who settled here might have dressed and fashioned their hair in this typically-Germanic style.

"Different people see different things at the cottage," said Chrissy. It is interesting just how similar the stories seem to be, with the common motif of an angry man murdering his family. There may have been a tremendous act of bloodshed at some point in the past, and this left residual energy that resonates into future time and space with its powerful imagery and sounds.

Investigation at Dudley Castle

On 30 July 2011, a public investigation into supernatural activity at Dudley Castle was held by PHI, which is the acronym for Paranormal Hauntings Investigations. They kindly invited me to observe and participate in the night's events.

PHI is headed by Sue Latham. She led the investigation at Dudley Castle, assisted by Chrissy, Dawn, Duane, Pete, Reg and Sarah. They each have different levels of psychic ability, whether sensing the presence of spirits, or identifying their names, origins and intentions. Many of them enter a trance-like state in which they seem to channel spirits. That is, they are temporarily "taken over" or "possessed".

This was a large public investigation, with around thirty to forty people in attendance. Dudley Castle employees were present at an early stage. It had been a lovely, warm July evening, and no clouds marred the night sky. The castle was eye-catching: a spotlight illuminated it and made it visible from much of the surrounding region.

Little wonder it is a local landmark. The Black Country is a historically-significant area of the West Midlands, with a proud heritage of industry and commerce; and at the heart of the Black Country is Dudley, watched over by its medieval castle. The structure marks one of the highest points in the region, and its views stretch for many miles. It was considered impregnable, and has never been captured by storm. It was a focus for local Royalist forces in the English Civil War, and withstood two sieges by Parliamentarians before surrendering in 1646. To prevent further resistance, the Parliamentarian army destroyed the keep, gateway and parts of the curtain wall, which were never fully restored in subsequent years. Before this mortal blow, it would have been an impressive sight on the hilltop: the keep was a huge rectangular structure, the corners reinforced by four towers, surrounded by two immensely sturdy walls and a moat - creating an impression of monolithic scale and strength.

An architecturally-beautiful manor house was built within the castle's walls, extravagantly redesigned on the command of Sir John Dudley in the 16th century. It was ravaged by fire in 1750. Now all are ruins.

Screams in the Undercroft

The Undercroft is a former crypt and storage area directly beneath the castle's old chapel. It is on ground level with the modern courtyard, not far from the castle's triple gateway, and is connected to the ruins of the manor buildings. "Real things are here in the Undercroft – they follow you round all night," Chrissy warned me.

It is a long rectangular room, with a curved, vaulted ceiling. The walls and ceiling are constructed from stone and bricks. There are lines of wooden benches across the room. At the end of the Undercroft is a wooden stage or platform, upon which there is a wooden chair – placed like a throne – with jumble and props all around, such as suits of armour, pikes, a wooden punishment stock, a tapestry. On each side of this stage are stone coffins, or sarcophaguses, lidless and empty; I could see where the stone had been shaped to create depressions for a corpse. One of these had been used for the burial of John de Somery, lord of Dudley, who died in 1321. On the ceiling were small lights around which I could see flies buzzing. *Are these the explanation for some of the orbs photographed in here*, I wondered. Cobwebs hung artfully from the ceiling, and the air was musty. But it did not feel claustrophobic, nor did I sense a negative atmosphere.

PHI is not the only group of supernatural enthusiasts to have been intimidated by the Undercroft. The WOLF research team was also "overwhelmed by a strong feeling of apprehensiveness" during their vigils.[18] They reported interesting results from trigger objects and séances conducted in this room. Gemma Woolridge, a former WOLF investigator, reported that, "My scariest experience was in the Undercroft. During a group séance a monk was apparently standing behind me, and I felt a burning heat spread across my shoulders. According to the medium the monk was chanting in Latin and the word 'striven' appeared, and I was being poked with a red-hot poker! The medium said that this was because I had some sins that I need to confess to myself - these

---

[18] ibid

have yet to become known to me! But I was incredibly scared and I don't scare that easily."[19]

The reports of spooky incidents go back decades. In 1962, the Undercroft was home to the zoo aquarium, and staff working here were disturbed by strange moans and groans, icy blasts of air, doors that opened and closed of their own accord, and footsteps which had no visible cause. Even further back, in 1953, a ghost hunt held by the Birmingham Psychic Research Society reported similar manifestations, with one person feeling a "light tap" on her shoulder.[20]

The first event of the night was a large group séance in the Undercroft. Everybody joined hands in a circle, the wooden benches having been removed to create a large open space. Inside this was an inner-circle, consisting of PHI staff, and within this was a K2 meter.

K2 meters are an alternative to more traditional EMF readers: they use a number of LEDs to measure the strength of an energy field instead of a numerical LCD screen. The intention is to monitor for abnormal fluctuations in electro-magnetic fields, said to signify

---

[19] Peter Drake, *Tales of Ghostly Horror: Real-life Encounters with the Supernatural*, 2010, pages 154-55.

[20] For further information: http://www.dudleycastle.org.uk/miscellaneous.html

ghostly activity. The K2 meter had brightly lit bulbs to indicate activity – a single green light was normal, with the flashing of further green lights or red lights indicating a surge in activity.

The lights were turned off, throwing this old room into darkness. I could see a small glimmer of light from the emergency exit beacon, and – strangely – bright small dots on a wall, almost like rain, which I later discovered were small luminous stickers.

The PHI members were leading the séance. They called out for things to make themselves known, or to create noises and smells. In the gloom it began to feel that the stones walls and ceiling were closer, that it was more confined. People said they could see things: they saw shadowy figures; little splashes of light that moved and zigzagged; snakes writhing on the floor; and something with white legs.

I observed these white legs; at first I could not explain it and it seemed damned peculiar – until I worked out these long, hazy stretches of white were probably reflected light from the exit sign, shining off the smooth floor. There have been reports of an apparition in the Undercroft and the visitor centre, where only the legs are visible. 'White Legs' is one of the more unusual apparitions reported at Dudley Castle.

A shadow moved on the other side of the room, but I saw it was only Pete, one of the PHI staff. My attention was brought to the left. "I thought I saw something moving then, from the corner of my eye," said the man next to me, in mild alarm.

The K2 meter went crazy with red lights. And one of the PHI staff screamed.

It was Duane, standing before me in the inner circle. His scream was deafening. He was having an attack of some sort; at first I thought it was a fit or seizure as he flailed out and fought to escape the efforts of his PHI team-mates to restrain him. Then I realised it was a trance, the first I have ever personally observed. A trance or possession is alleged to happen when a spirit attempts to take-over a suitable human host, usually a medium, as a vessel for communication.

While they may be common in television series such as 'Most Haunted,' it was a shock to see it played out before my eyes and in worryingly close proximity. We had been warned not to break the circle and relinquish hands, as this would render us vulnerable to unseen forces, so I could not exactly back away to safety. Torches flashed to illuminate the action. In muted light I could see Duane tussling with two or three people. He was asked questions: *Who are you? What is the year? Are you a soldier? Are you a knight?* The answers were indecipherable. After Duane recovered, he said he could not remember anything which had happened during his trance.

Seeking answers from the ghosts

We split into two smaller groups. My group moved to the castle's Visitor Centre, or museum, a large extended area fitted into the ground level of the manor ruins.

The visitor centre begins with a large circular room, named the 'zodiac room' by PHI staff: the walls are decorated with artwork scenes of the months of the year and descriptions of life in the past, with astronomical designs and the signs of the zodiac on the ceiling, and a large cardboard model of a castle in the middle of the room. A passage winds its way past faux-stone walls and information boards to another open room: here on display are disembodied, sculpted faces of the old lords of Dudley, looking down upon a display cabinet containing a scale model of Dudley Castle. A low, jagged archway leads into a larger room, now empty, where exhibitions and videos were previously shown; and from here is a ramp and short corridor leading to another empty room with a chequered floor – called the 'chequered room' by PHI and the 'chequer-board room' by castle employees. This was also previously used to exhibit historical items as part of the museum. The exit is from an adjacent room, formerly used as a gift shop.

In the castle's glory days, the Great Hall would have been above much of the modern Visitor Centre, including the zodiac room; and above the chequered room and former gift shop would have been the Solar, an area utilised as the lord's private chambers. The lower levels (i.e. the modern Visitor Centre) are medieval in origin.

We walked through the chequered room and connecting corridor, down the ramp to the exhibition room that was empty. There was a cool draft of air. I sat in a corner of the room writing notes, while the others held hands and stood in a circle. The lights were turned off.

The PHI team-member leading this séance was Reg, a short, stout man with a beard and a confident demeanour. He seemed to be acting as a medium reading the group, going through each person and asking them questions – or was he asking the spirits questions through these 'vessels'? Then Reg would provide the answers. People began reporting that they were cold, or that they felt drafts on their legs; Liz, a young woman from Birmingham, said she was being tickled on her neck and shoulders.

Meanwhile, Reg was starting to behave more aggressively. He made demands of the ghosts: "Make a noise – it *will* make a noise, it will show where it is! I *will* know your name, Sir, I will!...John...does John reside here?" He received answers from the spirits, apparently cowed by his threats: instead of John he received the name Philip, and the date was given as 1746. When a person suggested that there were spirits of children present he agreed: they were causing the drafts on people's legs by touching them and passing closely. Reg said that children had been hurt in this room.

Strangely enough, when I visited the castle some years ago there was an incident in this same part of the Visitor Centre, in which a child had been hurt by an item on display, a helmet or weapon I seem to remember. The injury was serious enough for a paramedic to be called in. On another occasion, my young son (who was only a toddler at the time) refused to go any further than the zodiac room, kicking and screaming just moments after he had been happy and smiling. Again, these are strange coincidences, and perhaps nothing more than that.

I was startled when a man named Stu fell into a trance-like state in the exhibition room. He was standing up, staring ahead, and swaying slightly as if he had fallen asleep. It was reminiscent of hypnotism.

In previous centuries this would have been called mesmerism, in which people were hypnotised (i.e. 'mesmerised') in order to open them up to contact with otherworldly forces. The way in which participants engage in a séance in a darkened room, listening to a medium's voice, may inadvertently put them into a hypnotic state if they truly accept the instructions of the medium. They lay themselves open to hypnotic suggestion and control. Mediums are probably not even aware they are doing this. The subconscious of willing participants might create messages from spirits, or they might believe they are being possessed by an alien personality which is actually a creation of their imagination. Hallucinations might be induced during this hypnotised state. Of course, there is the possibility that spiritual energies can only use a vessel for communication if the person's mental defences are lowered in this way.

Reg took the opportunity to question Stu as he remained in trance, hoping to snatch information from the spirit that seemed to invade Stu's body. He received the name Philip again, and discovered that Philip's age was 14 or 15 years. The trance did not last long. After recovering from his possession, Stu said he had "felt it trying to get in, but I wouldn't let it!"

Two ladies, named Jenny and Wendy, who I had met previously at a psychic fair at Dudley Castle, were increasingly drawn to the corridor and the chequered room. They were warned against it: "It's a bad place!" Nevertheless, it was our next destination.

The chequered room

There was a story from a castle employee who had worked in the Visitor Centre. He had never felt comfortable in these rooms and corridors. One day when walking through the chequered room he caught sight of a reflection of the floor behind him. He saw his legs moving, and behind them a second set of legs. It was White Legs. Twisting round in terror, he could not see anyone. No other employees were there, and the tourist attraction had not yet opened for the start of the day. He had no explanation.

Chrissy, a PHI team-member, had seemed excited by the so-called 'chequered room,' though reluctant to give anything away. Entering the room for the vigil, I found it dark and cool, and somehow less-ordinary than the exhibition room we had vacated. How much of this was down to my own expectations, I cannot say.

I participated in a séance in the chequered room. People began reporting strange smells, such as sulphur and fire. I had noticed curious aromas earlier that night, which were one person's bad-breath and another's rotten, stinky feet. Now I smelled something vile and oppressively disgusting, like the smell of excrement, i.e. human shit. This wafted past twice during the séance, slowly carrying from left to right, on each occasion coming from the direction of the connecting corridor to the museum. I kept this to myself, for fear of planting ideas in people's minds. Everyone seemed anxious enough without heightening the tension by saying that I could smell excrement, which is an indicator of demonic infestation.

Reg was leading the séance. He sensed the names Philip and Richard, and was sure that something "bad" was in that corridor, standing in the doorway and watching us. He asked me to leave the séance and stand close to the corridor, initially facing away from the doorway and then moving closer to within a few feet to look directly at it. I cannot say that I appreciated being placed in the way of spectral danger, making me likely to be the first person attacked, or maimed, or contaminated by that rotten stench, if the spirits decided to attack our gathering. "Do something to him," Reg pleaded with the spirits. "This man in the doorway is a writer and he doesn't believe in you. He wants you to do something. He will make you famous!" I was highly amused by this palaver. I stood there for several minutes, and did not experience anything unusual: there were no apparitions or cold fingers on my neck.

Returning to the séance circle, I could see that Reg was behaving strangely: he was much quieter, more intense. A small stone was thrown by someone - or something – and it pinged off the floor. I observed that Liz, the woman from Birmingham, had been awfully quiet for the past couple of minutes. When I asked if she was feeling all right, she did not answer, nor react when I poked her arm. She had blanked-out, and was taken out of the room to recover. I heard another woman acting bizarrely, mumbling and gasping in the dark.

Then all hell broke loose.

Reg went into a maniacal trance. He screamed and swore furiously, grappling with his PHI team-mate Duane. It was a blur of desperate struggle. It was much more violent than Duane's episode in the Undercroft. Everyone backed away in shock, in fear of being hit or kicked; one young woman was upset and clung to her mother.

It took the efforts of three people to restrain Reg. He began talking in an indecipherable manner. It was wild garbling. Then his speech became more recognisable, though strangely accented, and he answered questions with difficulty. It seemed that Reg was possessed by a Scottish knight named Edmond, who sought to protect us:

"Coming...something's coming....three....John...Richard... the alchemist! Down there......a...serpent....salamander... down....there....the alchemist!"

I was unsure whether to regard this as a horribly explosive possession, or as a spectacular piece of theatre. Were we really in the presence of a long-dead Scottish knight, who warned of a perilous evil that wished us harm?

I noted a discrepancy when he gave the year as 1614, and that his king was Robert Bruce - King Robert the Bruce of Scotland ruled from 1306-1329. This was incorrect information.

But, since Reg seemed to be struggling for breath at that point, I allowed him the benefit of the doubt.

Rummaging through the ruins

After a short break my small group reconvened at the manor ruins. We moved from section to section, from the old kitchens to the buttery and round this stony skeleton of what was once a magnificent manor house. Constructed within the castle walls, the buildings reached their zenith in the 16th century in the hands of Sir John Dudley, Duke of Northumberland; but they were irrevocably gutted by a fire that started on 24th July, 1750. The inferno was tremendous, and raged fiercely for three days; some reports suggest there were dozens of deaths.

People were asked for their impressions of the ruins. Some felt claustrophobic, or threatened, like they were being watched. However, I did not feel anything unusual and the majority of people seemed unperturbed.

There has always been an element of scepticism regarding the haunting of Dudley Castle. Looking back just a few decades to the 1980s, some viewed the ghost hunts organised by the castle authorities as money-making opportunities. I fear their reaction to the extravaganzas currently held at the castle. Such critics do not deny that the castle has supernatural inhabitants;

only that the ghostly heritage is being manipulated for financial gain.

Even firm believers have reservations about Dudley Castle, speculating that the ghosts are beginning to fade away. Christine Bosworth is the proprietor of Laura Elizabeth Crafts in Dudley town centre, and she is sensitive to spirits. She confirmed an old story of a spirit haunting the old kitchen – that of a young woman who died from serious injuries sustained from being scalded with boiling-hot water. During a visit to the castle, Christine stumbled across this spirit; but in a unique twist, she sensed that this young woman had in fact been deaf and dumb, and this disability was the cause of her accident as she had been unaware of her danger. It was not enough to assuage Christine's fears the castle has lost its edge: "Sometimes the place can be dead. I think the Grey Lady's gone – what's left there now is just residual [energy]. There's not much there."

Investigations by the WOLF Paranormal Research team have proved patchy: "It seemed on the night that the spiritual residents of Dudley Castle were a little bit tentative to make themselves known," said Paul Dyason, after one particularly quiet investigation. "But judging by the amount of orb activity in the photos they were certainly still with us!"

Paul has mixed feelings about the castle. He is concerned that activity has decreased because of overexposure; yet it has also provided him with what he calls "the best audible sound I have heard to date." It occurred during a WOLF public event in September 2008. Paul was with Dave Ball in the Visitor Centre: "We both clearly heard what I can only describe as a loud, long, and morose groan coming from the corridor behind us - the opposite direction from which we had entered the room."

This sound must have come from the long corridor which leads towards the exhibition room and the chequered room. "It was a groan, as loud and definite as I'm talking to you now," said Paul. "As soon as we heard it I shot down the corridor, and there was no one there. Dave walkie-talkied Simone [Taylor], and she said there was no one else anywhere near this area. Sensitive members of the team were getting activity that night. There were things roaming."

The Visitor Centre must be regarded as Dudley Castle's paranormal hotspot, due to the sheer number of reports of activity. "The museum has a very strong presence," said Liz Cormell, from WOLF.

To counter the sceptics and those with mixed feelings, there are a substantial number of firm believers who are certain that the castle and zoo are haunted. "Parts of Dudley Castle are the most haunted places I've been to," said Dawn Goding, a WOLF paranormal investigator. "I've seen the most activity there." Ghost-hunts are frequent and highly popular with the public.

Dr. David Riley is the chief presenter at Dudley Zoo and Castle, and has been a practicing clairvoyant for over twenty years worldwide: "From the first time I walked into Dudley Castle I knew it was a very active place as far as the paranormal is concerned. Not a day goes by that we don't get reports of something spiritual happening by visitors, and I often see during the day familiar spiritual faces at different points around the castle. I have now worked for Dudley Castle for over seven years and this building never disappoints!"

Back to the Undercroft

After the subdued response in the manor ruins, my small group moved back to the Undercroft. Another séance was held. A small, soft ball was place in the middle of the circle, and around it was sprinkled a thick circle of powder - in hope that the spirits could be persuaded to move the ball or to make imprints in the powder. If it were disturbed we would know. Alongside was placed a K2 meter. The lights were turned off. A long period of silence followed, broken only by Reg calling out to the spirits. We waited for the K2 meter to change, to indicate levels of activity by showing further green or red lights.

We waited. And waited.

Nothing happened.

Reg began taunting the spirits for their lack of interest. He made threats to a person named 'Mary,' obviously to provoke any entities that had an attachment to that name. There were sexually-orientated threats made to Mary. Females in the group began taunting the male spirits, besmirching their masculinity in a crass attempt to play upon 'sexism.' I wondered if ghosts cared about the 'gender war' or 'battle of the sexes' – though male spirits are famously interested in human females, a legacy of their corporeal desires.

This was unsuccessful in provoking activity. The powder was undisturbed, and the K2 meter had not flashed whatsoever – not even a single bulb flash. Reg was surprised: "I've never known it so quiet." It was in stark contrast to the rapid flashing earlier that night in the Undercroft. A few men reported that they had unusual pains in their backs. We were told by Reg that it was the spirits pushing us. I had been feeling an aching pain in my lower back for some time, and had attributed it to standing near-motionless for some length of time. However, many people believe that an unexplained pressure or heaviness in the back or kidney area is symptomatic of the presence of ghosts.

The men were ordered to leave the circle, leaving only the females. I sat further back, on the floor close to the stage. When I was caught in a flash of torchlight, a man jolted as he caught a glimpse of me sitting alone and cross-legged; I had to persuade him I was real.

There was nothing. No K2 activity, no noises, no trances.

Until we heard a stone hit the stage and rattle as it bounced off objects. "What the hell was that?!" I said. Later we heard another stone hitting the stage.

The stones could have fallen from the ceiling, but the noise seemed to suggest an amount of momentum and throwing force. I had a sense of something whistling past me. Someone in the room could have thrown it, a person who - like me - was not part of the séance and had their hands free. There were PHI staff frequently passing in and out of the room, and due to the darkness I had no real idea how many people were there, let alone *who* was there.

Dawn came into the Undercroft. She is a PHI staff member, and is considered a person who easily provokes the spirits resident in this room. Jenny soon fell into a violent trance. Along with her friend, Wendy, she had been drawn to the chequered room earlier that night. Wendy had been waiting for this moment all night, armed with a camcorder and a gleeful readiness to record Jenny's possession. It had previously been explained how on another occasion in the Undercroft, Jenny had entered a trance-like state: she had been screaming her lungs out, kicking frantically as if she were trying to walk very quickly. With no memory of the event, she heard about what happened from Wendy, who was hoping to catch another episode on camera.

Jenny now began her trance very quietly, and appeared to be asleep on her feet; then a barrage of screaming and swearing, almost like she was having a fit. She fell down and kicked out as her friends tried to restrain her. Someone said that she had been sick on the floor – "Don't tread in it!" - but I could not see it. Wendy had no time to record the incident, forgetting the camcorder as she tried to help her vulnerable friend.

Dawn experienced a similar attack minutes later, though it was much more visceral, with initial moments of muteness, vacancy, a 'tranced-out' state – followed by an outburst, and a slow recovery. During this session in the Undercroft, the K2 meter only flashed once – briefly, and softly. The room seemed dead to any paranormal activity.

***Chequered*-mate!**

The remaining investigators and members of the public gathered in the Visitor Centre to make the final push. It was now late into the night; several people had already left the castle grounds because they were tired. I felt utterly exhausted, and sitting in darkness only exacerbated my craving for sleep.

We all stood in the zodiac room, facing the doorway into the corridor that led further into the Visitor Centre - towards the exhibition room and the chequered room. A table was placed in the doorway, upon which the K2 meter was placed. It reminded me of an experiment from the 'Most Haunted: Live' investigation at Dudley Castle. In darkness we waited for flashing LEDs to indicate EMF activity. Sue Latham was leading the experiment, coaxing the spirits into showing themselves. The K2 meter went off, lighting up to its fullest indicators. The flash of green and then red shone brightly on the pale walls, creating an eerie effect.

Sue seemed to be in contact with a spirit. She asked for its name, making suggestions, and each time waiting for the K2 meter to light up in confirmation that it was the correct name. For no name did it flash. Until she said Francis, and it lit up. "So your name is Francis?" she queried. The K2 meter flashed again. By similar questioning she discovered that the spirit was a Father Francis. People said they could see something moving in the archway. They had been frightened of this place all night, and now felt they knew the name of the mysterious presence that had watched them and followed them.

It went quiet. The K2 meter was silent. "What's that, right by my face?" asked Sue. Then I could swear that I heard a blowing noise, swiftly followed by Sue screaming and leaping backwards. The K2 meter was going crazy.

She had reacted to something blowing in her face, which she felt was most likely this Father Francis. I have no concrete idea if another person made the blowing noise. After all, I was very tired. But I am sure that I heard *something* in those moments before Sue screamed.

We progressed down the much-feared corridor, stopping at each corner as the table and K2 meter were placed down and waiting for something to happen. Sue and others continued calling out. Another PHI team member played monastic music on her phone, hoping to encourage the spirits with familiar sounds. They were sure that the spirits were monks.

Just as the K2 meter surged to a high level I heard a stone bounce off the floor by the table. When torches were shone we could see a small pebble on the floor.

I was again cognisant of the fact that I could not account for every member of PHI or the castle employees in these corridors. They had come and gone all night. Any one could have thrown that stone in the darkness and padded away, the noise of their steps safely masked by exclamations of shock and wonderment from the investigators.

This slow trek culminated in an informal vigil in the chequered room. There was no formal séance, as most people (myself included) were just too tired. Sue and Dawn had an urge to lie down on the patterned floor, facing upwards, and they asked an overweight male from the group to lie down next to them. "I'm being drawn downwards, into the floor," said Sue, as she received negative sensations. "There's someone down there, they're lying down. They want me down there."

"Aren't there supposed to be people buried down here?" asked a random voice in the darkness.

Sue was getting weird feelings. "I've an urge to open my legs, to lie here and open them," she said. When the women rose from the floor, they acted on an urge to stand back-to-back; they said it was for protection, but Reg did not agree, perhaps implying some kind of lesbian sexual act associated with the stance. Maybe they were being influenced into adopting this stance.

Alchemy and occultism

There have been suggestions that occult rituals and orgies have taken place at the castle, perhaps in the chequered room. The terms 'salamander' and 'alchemist' were often used by the PHI team, I believe in reference to these practices.

There is a suggestion that the 'alchemist' at Dudley Castle is a man called Dud Dudley, who during his lifetime attempted to turn metal into gold. Others feel that high-ranking people from the local area were involved in the dark arts here.

According to Wikipedia:

> *"Alchemy is an ancient tradition, the primary objective of which was the creation of the mythical "philosopher's stone," which was said to be capable of turning base metals into gold or silver, and also act as an elixir of life that would confer youth and immortality upon its user. Alchemy can be viewed as a protoscience, a precursor to modern chemistry, having provided procedures, equipment, and terminology that are still in use. However, alchemy also included various non-scientific mythological, religious, and spiritual concepts, theories and practices."*[21]

Alchemy was popular in certain circles in Renaissance England, with influential practitioners such as Dr. John Dee (astrologer to Queen Elizabeth I) also involved in occult practices. Dr. Dee was a highly intelligent man, who combined sorcery, necromancy and science in his endeavours, and is notorious for allegedly raising the spirit of a deceased woman in a churchyard on a night of

---

[21] http://en.wikipedia.org/wiki/Alchemy

the full moon. He experimented with talking boards (a less-refined version of a Ouija board) to communicate with lower elemental forces; and used crystal balls to look into unearthly realms.

The real Dud Dudley was a bastard son of the baron of Dudley. In the 17th century, he was intimately involved in kick-starting the Industrial Revolution in the town of Dudley with his experiments in metallurgy and chemistry. A man with his interests would have been regarded as an alchemist, and considering his family links to Dudley Castle (he also fought as a Royalist during the English Civil War, with local forces based at the castle) there is every possibility he conducted experiments here.

Interestingly, the salamander is a mythical creature, depicted as a lizard-like creature with an affinity to fire and sometimes with magical powers. It had an influential role in the occult, and was discussed by key alchemists such as Paracelsus. It is strongly linked to the Dudley region: "The salamander became the traditional emblem of the smith, and thus appears in a number of civic arms to symbolise local metal-working industries. It appears in the arms of Dudley Metropolitan Borough Council, as well as the old County Borough Council."[22]

---

[22]http://en.wikipedia.org/wiki/Salamander_(legendary_creature)

Could PHI and other paranormal investigators be sensitive to the aftermath of experiments with witchcraft and alchemy, carried out by some of the most influential people in Dudley's past? These strange coincidences suggest there might be more to Dudley Castle than meets the eye.

Further information

http://www.dudleyzoo.org.uk/
(Official website for Dudley Zoological Gardens and Castle)

http://www.dudleycastle.org.uk/
(Website for 'The Friends of Dudley Castle')

http://www.phinights.moonfruit.com/
(Website for PHI, Paranormal Hauntings Investigations)

http://www.wolf-rs.co.uk/paranormal/investigation_dudley_castle.html
(Details of WOLF investigation at Dudley Castle)

WHITE LADIES PRIORY

Interview with Alex Oldman

Many visitors to White Ladies Priory have sensed an eerie presence. Jane, a young woman from Wolverhampton, said: "I've had the feeling that I'm being watched when I go into the ruins, it's scary and makes you tremble. I haven't seen anything, I've just felt it. And I didn't like it." There are rumours of ghostly chanting, prayers and songs.

Alex Oldman has vivid memories of the priory:

"One night when he was younger my dad was camping there with a friend when he saw something. It was a ghost of woman wearing all white, and he knew it was a nun. It was looking right at them, and was walking towards them, so they got up and ran away. I used to live nearby when I was a kid, so I was interested in the story he told me. When I was a teenager I had a sudden, weird urge to cycle there; it was really late, around 3am, and even later by the time I got there. I didn't see anything at the priory. When I got on my bike and started cycling I could see a strange light ahead; it was bright and was getting closer. It was really close, then it stopped. When I heard people get out and start speaking to me I realised it was a

police car, and it was coppers talking to me, not ghosts."

All that remains of White Ladies Priory are ruins. It was built in the grounds of a medieval nunnery in the 12th century, just north of Albrighton, and close to the city of Wolverhampton. Neighbouring landmarks are Boscobel House and Chillington Hall – both of which are considered to be haunted. The land on which the priory stands was possibly a hub for religion and spirituality long before recorded history. Little wonder some ascribe a strange mystical quality to this tiny spot in the Shropshire countryside.

There is a legend that Queen Guinevere (wife of King Arthur) retired here to become a nun. An interesting feature of White Ladies Priory's medieval history is the presence of a statue of the Virgin Mary: it was reputedly made of fine white marble and possessed magical powers, including the ability to prophesise doom and misfortunes. It stood at the priory for several centuries until 1536, when the Reformation hit. The priory was looted by the king's troops and at this point the statue disappeared from all public knowledge.

DENNY ABBEY

Interview with Dawn Goding

There are many stories of ghosts in the fenlands of Cambridgeshire. Underground tunnels at monastic sites in this region are said to be inhabited by unearthly forces. The disembodied spirits of monks wander the empty shells of their priories; and ethereal singing is sometimes heard at night, eerily like monastic chanting, and carried on the winds that coil over this countryside.

Denny Abbey is reputedly haunted. A former abbey near Waterbeach, it is six miles north of Cambridge in Cambridgeshire, England.[23] The site, on an ancient road between Cambridge and Ely, was settled by farmers as early as the Roman period. In the 1150s, a group of Benedictine monks arrived from nearby Ely, and in 1159 they finished construction on Denny Priory. Only the crossing and transepts remain of these original buildings.

In 1169, the site came into the possession of the Knights Templar. This was a military-religious order that grew to prominence in the Crusades, accruing wealth and power much to the envy of secular authorities. In

---

[23] http://en.wikipedia.org/wiki/Denny_Abbey

1307, the Templars were accused of witchcraft and heresy: they came under attack over much of Western Europe, and, in 1308, King Edward III confiscated the priory and awarded it to the Knights Hospitaller, another crusading order. It was consequently given to Franciscan nuns – the Order of St. Clare – in 1377, and expanded into an abbey. It became a large, bustling place, an administrative centre for local farming. It closed in 1539 after the monasteries were dissolved by King Henry VIII. Denny Abbey and its lands passed into private ownership, being adapted for agricultural use.

The abbey has decayed since it heyday. Its caretakers boldly describe it as "an architectural jigsaw of windows, blocked doorways and arches."[24] "It's almost a ruin, it's all open," said Dawn Goding, who visited the abbey for a paranormal investigation with WOLF. Restoration works took place in the 1960s, and the ruins are now open to the public.

Dawn was excited by unexplained activity during her vigil at Denny Abbey: "There was a dark figure. In the room upstairs, we were doing a circle [séance] but not calling out; I looked at Dave and I saw a mysterious figure behind him. It was raining, and dark. Simone asked, "Can you see that?" She described the same thing I saw – a dark hooded figure. I felt that it was a man

---

[24] http://www.dennyfarmlandmuseum.org.uk

wearing a cloak; he was six or seven feet tall. And he was right behind Dave. No one else saw it; Dave didn't see it. And [at the time] no one else felt it or sensed it."

The WOLF investigators seemed to agree that religious faith was a factor in seeing this apparition and interpreting its purpose: "Someone thought it was an angel," said Dawn, "while others, like Liz [Cormell], told us it wasn't evil. Dave said he had been religious when he was younger, but now he's ambivalent about religion, hence he was not picking up on it."

There was another incident which spooked the WOLF team. It occurred on a walkway, possibly the crossing, one of the abbey's original and oldest structures. "We were freezing, having a coffee," Dawn said. "Then we heard some footsteps on a walkway on the top landing. But there was no one up there. We were all downstairs. They were quite heavy footsteps. Everybody heard them. I heard four or five steps, over a few seconds. There were motion sensors up there, and they didn't go off." There have been unexplained bangs, rapping and footsteps upstairs during investigations by other teams, and in one instance a number of people felt the floor vibrating, so this is recurrent phenomenon.

Animals in nearby fields are supposed to act defensively in the evening, aware of some strange presence, according to local people. Even before a pair of wells was excavated at Denny Abbey, people could hear the sounds of a well being used. There are traditions that tell of giant eels snaking through tunnels beneath the abbey.

Other paranormal researchers have encountered the spirits or energies of monks, and even a German prisoner-of-war who had escaped captivity and hidden at the abbey ruins during the Second World War. Some have suddenly fallen ill or become violently sick for no obvious reason. Electronic voice phenomenon (EVP) has been picked up.

SENSING THE SUPERNATURAL

A selection of people with psychic abilities was asked: What does it feel like when you sense supernatural energies? Whether communicating with entities, or encountering an apparition, how would you best describe it? Here are a number of their answers.

> *"It's just like when a real person is standing behind you, you know they're there; if they're not real you just don't always look to see! I don't feel any pressure in my head; it's more like watching a film in your head!"*
>
> - Chrissy, investigator for PHI

> *"I'm actually claircogniscent, which means things pop into my head as if they were my own thoughts. The best way to describe this is, if I were to ask you your name you would be able to answer without thinking about it. I give answers from spirits in much the same way, I think. I do occasionally get things passed to me when I'm not "switched on" or looking for it, but I have learnt to ignore it if I'm not*

interested at that time. Sometimes it can be distracting but enlightening at the same time."

- Liz Cormell, WOLF claircogient

"It's a bit difficult to put it into words. I tend to try to describe it in physiological terms: if I am in an area that reports as being haunted, I can often get a light kind of 'fuzzy' feel in my head. I know how this sounds, but I don't know how else to describe it! I certainly don't get anything to the degree of, "Oh there's a spirit man standing over there," or anything like that. I just feel that what I experience is caused simply due to the fact that there may be an energy change in the atmosphere; even I can't interpret what has caused that change. In the past I have wondered if this is psychological, perhaps, as knowing somewhere is haunted may be affecting me. I don't know. The jury is still out."

- Paul Dyason, WOLF paranormal investigator and data analyst

"People's hands can go limp, or they can get the shakes. It's like when someone's standing behind you - you can sense them there but can't see them. The heart starts dropping, you can be hot or cold.

They can also start transforming, they're being used to channel things."

- Sue Latham, medium and psychic for PHI

"I'm not a psychic, I'm just sensitive to certain things. When you die, an energy is left behind. This energy is your soul. No energy ever truly disappears. [This energy is what you can sense or feel.] When you can sense things, there's a pressure in your head and in your heart. When it happens - the hairs on your arms! ... I've had it for years: they talk to me, they work with thoughts. The thoughts I get I would never have expected. I was on holiday with my family in France and we were in the countryside when I could suddenly see German soldiers shooting their guns; my family couldn't see it and they just said, "Oh no, she's at it again!""

- Christine Bosworth, proprietor of Laura Elizabeth Crafts, Dudley

"I'm only starting to do this, I can feel changes in the atmosphere, and I'm starting to sense things."

- Liz, from Birmingham

"I don't believe these mediums and spiritualists and babas, they're just making it up. They say they can speak to your dead loved ones, tell your future, see ghosts and everything; but I don't believe them. They're after money from gullible idiots who're desperate to believe things and feel better about how miserable life really is. Maybe the mediums believe it, too. They say they can feel things - it hurts in their head or in their chests, or the angels tell them things – urgh! They're imagining it, or it's just normal aches and pains. Unless I see it myself, or feel it myself, I'll never, ever believe it. I'm a strong believer in disbelieving!"

- Roger Wakelin, tradesman

"If you meditated you'd develop a [psychic] sense. I'm just starting to become sensitive. It takes time. It can be very comforting: one day I happened to hear my dad's voice, and without thinking I said "Hi, Dad." I had goose-pimples."

- Nancy Eccleston, from Canada

"It's like a pressure when I sense something, at the front of my head, between my eyes – I feel it there."

- Simone Taylor, WOLF co-founder

GREEN MAN ENTRY

Green Man Entry is an old, narrow passageway in Dudley, a large town in the West Midlands, England. "I've heard that it's haunted and there's some kind of poltergeist activity," said Roger Wakelin, a local tradesman. "Sometimes stones are thrown at people who walk down there, when no one else is around. And dental nurses who work next door, when they walk down the alley they say they sometimes have their bums pinched. They turn around ready to go mad and shout, and there's no one there. They said it didn't feel malicious, but you never know!"

The passageway is located in one of the oldest parts of Dudley, opposite St. Edmund's Church on Castle Street. It runs through a single row of well-kept buildings, near to Dudley Castle. It is situated on land that was probably originally part of the church's cemetery. The entry gains its name from the Green Man public house, which operated next to the passage for nearly two hundred years. After opening in the 1790s, it closed in 1975. In previous years it had been a home-brew house. Local townspeople recollect that it was a small pub, very cosy and old-fashioned. Above the entrance to Green Man Alley is a sculpture relief which keeps to the traditional design of a Green Man: a face bursting from leaves, with branches and vines spewing from his mouth and nostrils.[25]

Photographs of the Green Man pub in its 20th century pomp show that it has barely changed in appearance.[26] The exteriors remain basically the same. The pub has since been converted to offices but the entry is still used as a passage to the rear car park. It is not a safe or secure passageway: in January 2011, there were reports of assaults on women taking place in Green Man Entry. A lady was robbed and another was thrown against the wall; one person said that her assailant had placed his hand between her legs. This sounds similar to the paranormal activity detailed by Roger, in terms of the sexual element.

Investigations at Green Man Entry have been in small number. Not all local paranormal groups seem aware of its existence, and the town's ghost walks seem to be the sole repository of information regarding its supernatural charms. Among the phenomenon experienced by investigators are orbs and the sounds of faint footsteps. Tall figures have been spotted mysteriously watching investigators from the office's windows, despite all buildings being shut and empty during the late hours.

---

[25] http://www.a4a.com/greenmanreliefsc.html

[26] http://www.flickr.com/photos/24112096@N02/4502460825

It is interesting to ponder the significance of the Green Man imagery: was it merely an aesthetic choice or indicative of some symbolic purpose based on the location? It was a popular name for a pub in England, so it might not mean anything. The Green Man is an ancient pagan symbol for rebirth and regeneration. It is a strongly associated with the end of winter and the beginning of spring, the return of growth and nature's rebirth. The Green Man is utilised as a decorative architectural object in carvings, sculptures and artwork, and it is frequently found in churches and older buildings: for instance, there is a carving of the Green Man on a pillar in the crypt at Canterbury Cathedral, the seat of Christianity in England for a thousand years.

JIP, THE PROPHETIC DOG

Interview with Kirsty Law

Precognition can be described as "a type of extrasensory perception that would involve the acquisition or effect of future information that cannot be deduced from presently available and normally acquired sense-based information or laws of physics and/or nature."[27] It is the ability to visualise an event before it occurs, to look into the future. Premonitions are an emotional sense or feeling that something is going to happen, and are more generic.

Almost every person has experienced this, whether they realise it or not. Like the sense that someone is staring at you, it is something quite common but not recognised as an extrasensory perception. Often you will get a sudden thought of someone, and moments later receive a phone call or text message from that same person. You may randomly think of a person you have not seen for several years, and meet them in the street apparently by chance days later. Many people are convinced that dreams have given them forewarning of the deaths of family members or close friends, people

---

[27] http://en.wikipedia.org/wiki/Precognition

who later die unexpectedly. There have been cases of people getting an inexplicable and overpowering sense of dread or impending peril, changing their travel plans or other decisions and thereby avoiding disasters such as crashes and terrorist attacks. Airplanes and trains that suffer crashes are said to statistically carry fewer passengers that normal. Some people seem to sense they are going to die; they exhibit changes in behaviour such as sudden calm or unanticipated expressions of love to family members prior to their deaths.

Many of these elements feature in the build-up to the terrorist attacks that occurred on 11th September 2001, in New York City, U.S.A. The wife of a victim reports that he had behaved strangely for months: he instinctively felt that he was going to die soon, and at a family gathering he mentioned the possibility of another terrorist attack on the World Trade Centre (after a 1993 bombing), discussing escape routes with his brother.[28] As he prepared to leave for work on the morning of 11 September he suffered an attack of vertigo, and despite his wife's pleas to remain at home, he dutifully – and tragically – set off for his commute into New York. Many people claim they had prophetic dreams prior to the

[28] http://www.dailymail.co.uk/news/article-1310994/The-9-11-victims-foresaw-deaths-New-book-claims-victims-premonitions-atrocity.html

9/11 terrorist attacks. Some describe dreams in which they were standing in tall buildings that were shaking violently, warning people to escape but they do not listen or run in the wrong direction, and then the dreamer flees to a safe distance and watches the tall building collapse. Some dreamt of watching a cloud of dust and stones rushing towards them and being trapped in this cloud, unable to breathe. There are innumerable examples.

One of the most famous examples of precognition involved the sinking of the Titanic in April 1912. Just fourteen years earlier an author named Morgan Robertson wrote a novel about an unsinkable ocean liner named Titan which sinks after hitting an iceberg one April night on its maiden voyage. Despite the avowal of sceptics that it was pure coincidence, many believe the author's ideas must have stemmed from subconscious glimpses into the future.

There are prophets such as Nostradamus who claim to see more clearly into the future, again through dreams and visions. An altered state of consciousness or perception seems to be a trigger.

It is not only humans that experience precognition and premonitions. Animals are believed to have this ability. It is part of ancient folklore that dogs can foretell natural phenomena such as earthquakes, and there is much anecdotal evidence that animals become noticeably agitated or exhibit strange behaviour prior an earthquake.[29] A number of explanations have been offered, such as animals sensing gas escaping from the earth, perhaps alerted by changes in electrical fields or low-frequency vibrations. Parapsychology also speculates that animals might in some unexplained way have the ability to see the future. If they have a different state of consciousness and perception of time to humans, animals could experience a wider segment of the space-time continuum. That is, animals might perceive a broader spectrum of past-present-future than humans might, whether by seconds, minutes or hours. It is entirely feasible given developments in the theory of quantum physics, and experiments at CERN, the giant particle accelerator near Geneva, Switzerland, which suggest that the speed of light can be exceeded, thus time or the observation of events in space-time may not be a constant.

There were reports of strange animal behaviour in England during the Second World War. Animals such as dogs would act with fear and agitation prior to aerial bombing raids, without the possibility of hearing aircraft or feeling vibrations from their engines. One particularly relevant story came from Kirsty Law, a young woman from the West Midlands whose grandparents were

---

[29] http://animalsandearthquakes.com/etho-geo.htm

warned of impending danger by their family pet during The Blitz.

The Blitz (September 1940 – May 1941) marked the height of Germany's assault on Britain in the Second World War. Military and industrial centres were strategically attacked by the German air force. The major cities were targeted for heavy and prolonged bombardment – at one point the city of London was under attack for 76 consecutive nights, with more than a million houses destroyed and over 20,000 civilians killed. Another of Kirsty Law's relations had been a fire-watcher for a hospital in London during the Blitz; she remarked that it seemed that the entire city on fire, watching bomb after bomb hit, including incendiary bombs, and she could see from her high spot on the hospital roof the blazes raging in every direction for miles. Cities such as Hull, Bristol, Southampton, Manchester and Liverpool were hit by the Luftwaffe's raids.[30]

The West Midlands was heavily targeted due to its density of manufacturing, munitions factories and the presence of Spitfire and tank production. There was severe damage in places like Birmingham, and the centre of Coventry was almost completely obliterated. This destruction inevitably spread into surrounding suburbs.

---

[30] http://en.wikipedia.org/wiki/The_blitz

Kirsty Law recollected one seemingly ordinary evening in 1942, when her grandparents were about to go to bed: "Their dog, Jip, had always went upstairs with them to bed without fail since they had him as a puppy. But this one night he absolutely refused to go upstairs. He just would not go! My granddad tried picking him up to carry him, but Jip was having none of it – he was snarling, pulling away, jumping out of his arms, refusing to go upstairs. This was unusual, but they just thought he was being stupid. They gave up and left him downstairs, while they went to bed. In the early hours of the morning my nan woke up. She could hear a plane overhead, with noisy engines; and she could hear more planes. Then there was an explosion."

That night the German air force launched a raid on the West Midlands. Anyone watching from the nearby hills would have seen flames across the region from where their bombs had hit, and staccato light from the combat in the skies. The Germans were pursued by British fighters, who sought to shoot them down before they could escape. One of the German aircraft was flying over the area where Kirsty's grandparents lived when it dropped its remaining munitions, in order to lighten its weight and fly faster. The bomb landed directly in the middle of the road outside Kirsty's grandparents' house.

There was devastation: two semi-detached houses across the road were destroyed by the blast. All but one of the occupants survived, a woman who was too frightened to leave her bed and join family as they fled. She cowered in terror beneath her pillow and blankets, and was later found dead in her bed, suffocated as masonry fell on her.

The property belonging to Kirsty's grandparents suffered extensive damage: "Nan and Granddad heard and felt the bomb blast," she said. "It must have been huge. The blast made the roof collapse and it badly damaged the ceiling; it would have fallen in on them as they lay in bed, too quickly for them to get out, if not for an oaken wardrobe. It was a big, tall oaken double wardrobe, old-fashioned and strong. It acted as a roof support as the roof fell in. My nan and granddad saw the ceiling start to bow with the weight of the collapsed roof on it. My granddad shouted to get out. The wardrobe allowed them just enough time to get out of the bed, get downstairs and grab the dog and get out. Then it all fell down."

It is mystifying how Jip knew something was going to happen that night and refused to go upstairs where the danger was greatest. Kirsty suggested the dog had some sort of animal extrasensory perception (ESP). Like animals fleeing a forest fire or acting bizarrely before an earthquake, Jip had a premonition. How else could it have known?

They were forced to live downstairs in their shattered abode for months. With war-time demands on men and materials there was nothing available to repair the extensive damage. People in the street felt fortunate that the damage was not worse or more widely-spread. At least it had only been a single bomb, and the majority had survived. Kirsty's grandparents told her how lucky they were to have placed the sturdy oak wardrobe in just the right place, without which they would almost certainly have died.

They thought how utterly bizarre and coincidental was Jip's refusal to go upstairs, hours before the explosion: "Granddad said the next time the dog refuses to go upstairs, we all sleep downstairs!"

LITTLEDEAN HALL

Chronicle of a paranormal landmark

One of the most haunted houses in England is Littledean Hall. No doubt this is partially due to its status as the oldest inhabited dwelling in the country – it has been continuously lived-in since the arrival of the Anglo-Saxons in the 5th century. But there is something more disturbing at Littledean Hall than mere echoes of the past, something more malevolent and dangerous.

The hall was built by Saxons in the 5th or perhaps 6th century in the village of Littledean, in the Forest of Dean, Gloucestershire. The Saxons were not the first people to settle at this location: there are traces of Neolithic and Roman roads, and the remains of a Roman temple have been discovered in the grounds. The Romans adapted an existing Celtic shrine which venerated Sabrina, goddess of the River Severn, which flows a short distance away. The site would have mystical significance to the Celts, as it possesses a springhead and overlooks a horseshoe bend of the river as it meanders through a valley, flanked by high hills. Archaeological remains found at the temple are dated from the late Mesolithic through to the Bronze Age.

In the cellar of Littledean Hall there is evidence of its original Saxon hall, which was an open living space; this would have been continually improved and expanded by successive generations, until it was finally converted to a Norman hall with an upper floor and Undercroft for storage. The 'lords of Dene' ruled the local area from this residence after the Conquest; they are first mentioned in written records from the year 1080. There is a tradition of incorporating older elements when fashioning a new dwelling at Littledean Hall: several fragments of Roman masonry have been found in the surviving part of the Saxon dwelling; and many older sections were retained after a substantial redesign in 1612 transformed the hall into a Jacobean structure.

The Jacobean aesthetic of Littledean Hall has survived the centuries. It presents an austere facade to visitors. "I didn't like the building, it looked weird," said Kirsty Law, a visitor to the hall. "You can't see it from the road, it's kind of hidden away. It's got the feeling of being old – the actual site, not just the building. It's a strange place. Mainly because it's old. There are a lot of windows in the hall, which makes it seem creepy. They give you the impression of eyes. There are too many windows; there don't seem to be enough rooms inside to account for all of them. It makes you think there might be hidden rooms!"

Kirsty visited Littledean Hall on an archaeological field-trip with her college. The building is considered archaeologically important due to its long history of human habitation, having been continually lived-in since the 5th century or perhaps much earlier, if considering the site's Celtic and Roman roots.

She gave an interview on her unsettling experience:

"I didn't know it was haunted, I had no expectations. My group went in the bits that were Saxon, and it didn't feel particularly creepy. It was under the house, and just seemed like an old cellar. It's just a bit dark. There were some people complaining and saying, "I don't like it!" I didn't really see anything down there.

"On the tour they told us that the bedroom upstairs was haunted. They showed us around; it had a four-poster bed, and wooden panelling, I think. I think it was the Rose room. They didn't say what haunted it. [There is a story of an illegitimate baby murdered and hidden behind a secret panel in this room.] *But I didn't feel anything at all in the bedroom. My friend Brendan was pretending that he could sense stuff in there – "It's creepy!" he said – but it didn't feel bad. It was nice and sunny in there.*

"Across from this room was another one. The tour went in there. Not many people went in, though. Most of them just had a quick look and then left. Me and Brendan were at the back, so we waited

for everyone else to leave. There was a single bed in the room, and a red military jacket on a doll, like a dress-making doll; I think the room was blue. They never told us the room was haunted; there was no mention of it.

"Out of all the rooms I saw, this was the one room I didn't like. It had an oppressive atmosphere, it was horrible. It made me feel uncomfortable, and it felt nasty. The room felt unwelcoming, if you know what I mean. It was a bright room, not dark; it wasn't nasty in itself, it was nicely decorated and not cluttered. I didn't want to go into the room too far; I stayed close to the doorway. I suppose it was the feeling that someone was in the room and you couldn't see them, and they didn't want you in there. I would not have wanted to stay in there by myself!

"Brendan didn't like it, and he seemed genuine this time. He said it seemed weird in there; he didn't like it and wanted to get out. When we came out of the room, it felt normal again. I never pick up on anything in so-called haunted places. But I did in this room.

"They gave us a guide to Littledean Hall, and after we left I read a story about this bedroom. People have seen a woman looking out of a window in this room, when no one was supposed to be in here.

One day a person came in and saw a woman looking out of the window. She was in period costume, and they thought she was a tour guide. She wore a dress, which was big and billowing on the bottom, like some sort of costume you'd get in the George III-period, with hoops underneath the petticoat. The woman's back was turned towards the window, and when she turned around to look at the person they could see that she had no eyes."

The place where Kirsty sensed a forbidding presence was the Blue room. This is considered one of the most paranormally-active and unpleasant of all the rooms and spaces at Littledean Hall. In recent years, an owner of the house reported a disturbing incident that occurred as he slept in a bedroom, very possibly the Blue room. He was woken one night by his dog's hysterical barking, and fearful of an intruder he sat up in bed. He was wide awake. Inexplicably he had a sensation of being sharply shoved in the back. Then he was forcibly pushed across the bed. After recovering, he could not find anyone else in the room.

This is reminiscent of another incident, reported by a regimental sergeant major billeted at Littledean Hall during the Second World War: "He was sleeping in an upstairs room, when on one occasion at 2am he was awakened by a slap across his face. Opening his eyes, he saw a tall lady holding a monkey which was touching his face. When he put the light on, they vanished."[31] No wonder the Blue room is considered hazardous to sleep in.

The spectral lady that haunts the Blue room is certainly a recurrent feature. A sighting of this apparition by a woman from Barnstaple corroborates earlier stories: "Just leaving the bedroom, I was conscious of someone behind me so I turned around and saw what I can only describe as an unusual pillar of light or source of power. There was nothing defined about it, and yet as I stared I had the impression of a young woman looking out of the right-hand window. Somehow I knew she was unhappy."[32] She sensed that the dress was blue. After leaving the room and entering the grounds, the visitor looked up at the Blue room's window and was shocked to see the same female ghost looking out.

Stories of the building's unearthly denizens have circulated since the 16th century. They include tales of a ghostly gardener who tends the vegetation outside; and a monk or priest, who has been seen near a priest-hole hidden behind panelling. There is the famous phantom bloodstain, originally blood which pooled on the dining

---

[31] See Roy Harley Lewis, *Ghosts, Hauntings and the Supernatural World*, 1991, page 134

[32] ibid

hall floor from the corpses of Royalist officers impaled and killed during a violent attack by Parliamentarian forces during the English Civil War; the blood cannot be permanently removed, so the story goes, as it periodically re-appears at the same spot no matter how many times it is washed away or even if the floorboards are replaced.

A visitor to the hall's cellar – once a Saxon hall - reported hearing sounds of everyday life here, such as the noise of music, of dogs and horses, of children playing, and the sounds of a fire crackling. She thought it was a recording played on loudspeakers as part of a tour, until she was told there were no loudspeakers in the cellar. Other visitors to the cellar with clairaudient abilities have been aware of unseen people talking all around them, while this has been inaudible to colleagues.

An elderly housekeeper had a horrifying experience in the 1960s: "We had three Labradors, a mother and a puppy and a third which suffered from epileptic fits. On one occasion, she went up the backstairs into the corridor which is about twenty feet long. She took the dogs with her, and just as they were about to move down the corridor, she was conscious of a bang from the door opening on to the courtyard downstairs. At that moment, all three dogs began whining with fear, foaming at the mouth and two went into fits. A moment later she felt a shudder through her and then suddenly all the doors in the corridor opened simultaneously."[33]

Randolph Liebeck called Littledean Hall 'the most haunted house in England,' and published an article on the location in Fate Magazine in October 1997.[34] It is highly recommended reading for anyone interested in the activity at this ancient site. He described some of the paranormal activity experienced at the house since the 1950s:

> *"Some of the documented auditory phenomena included screams, clashing swords, pistol shots, rappings, and slamming doors. Among the olfactory phenomena were unattributable odours of decaying flesh, burning toast, and roses. Visual phenomena included animated gray-and-black mists, light orbs, and apparitions. Among the latter were a monk, Royalist soldiers, two brothers who shot each other over a woman, and the spirit of a young servant who murdered his master in 1774 and was subsequently executed. Some witnesses have reported dizziness, nausea, palpitations, encounters with psychic cold spots, and an almost*

---

[33] See Roy Harley Lewis, *Ghosts, Hauntings and the Supernatural World*, 1991, page 132

[34] http://www.myspace.com/blueridgeparanormal/blog/307555793

overwhelming sense of a presence. People have also been shoved, jerked, or punched by unseen hands. It isn't just two-legged beings who have noticed something unusual. Dogs at the manor have gone into unprovoked fits, foaming at the mouth and snapping at invisible intruders. Chairs, tables, and wall hangings in the manor have been mysteriously rearranged and overturned. Flowers in vases have been regularly found shredded and tossed about. Doors open and close on their own initiative. Various objects are playfully hidden and returned."[35]

A former hostess at Littledean Hall reported being enveloped by a dark cloud. It was in 1993, and she told Liebeck how she had been in the old stables when a "black sort of mist" came from a corner of a wall: "It formed into a large, dark, cloudlike mass and wrapped itself around me, and I couldn't do anything about it. I tried, but I couldn't move. I was actually physically restrained. I don't know for sure how long it lasted, but the next thing I knew I was pushed out of it, like you would push a person away, and I got out of there."[36]

---

[35]http://www.myspace.com/blueridgeparanormal/blog/307555793

[36] ibid

In 1996 Liebeck and a team of paranormal researchers (including, among others, a priest, a clairvoyant and parapsychologist) were brought in to Littledean Hall after a cleansing of the house had failed and apparently worsened the tense situation. The Liebeck investigation used much of the same equipment that has become the staple of modern paranormal research: night-vision cameras, EMF meters, motion detectors. The clairvoyant picked up activity in the house, and there were worries about people's safety. It was suggested that the house rests on the intersection of five ley lines (these are mystical alignments which can supposedly alter energy fields, often found at sacred or historical sites or along ancient pathways).

Unfortunately, the equipment did not monitor any substantial unexplained activity. There was one electrical anomaly discovered, apparently suspended at a height of six feet in a space between two rooms. After a clearing ritual was conducted to exorcise the house, the band of electrical interference had disappeared. The atmosphere had changed in the house, which now felt more positive and rather less threatening.

Some people disagree with the notion that the house can be permanently cleansed of its supernatural emanations. Like with the floorboards in the dining hall, the blood will always return. There are suggestions that whatever is at this location (with a history of mysticism and human habitation that spans millennia,) it cannot be stopped or driven away. Perhaps the intersection of ley lines replenishes its energy. For some, Littledean Hall is a "bad place," or an "evil place," a place which contains many different presences but ruled by a single dominant overlord, a negative entity which drains people. People can become sick after spending time here: a previous owner has reported sensing a malevolent influence that envelops the house, radiating a "toxic atmosphere" that causes physical illness and depression.

Whether or not there is "evil" at Littledean Hall, it is obvious that the place has a baleful influence on visitors and inhabitants.

Also by Peter Drake

Tales of Ghostly Horror: Real-life Encounters with the Supernatural

Feel a profound sense of dread at the ghostly horrors that scratch at the surface of our world. Discover frightening true accounts of poltergeists, apparitions and malevolent entities, and explore some of England's most fearsome haunted locations with WOLF ('World Oneiric Life Force'), a paranormal research & investigation team. Alongside locations made famous by the likes of TV series 'Most Haunted' are fresh additions to supernatural lore. The twenty-three stories include:

The Galleries of Justice — Woodchester Mansion

The Station Hotel — The Ancient Ram Inn

The Hellfire Caves — Edinburgh Vaults

The Theatre on the Steps — Middleton Hall

The Pervy Poltergeist — and more!

AVAILABLE TO BUY IN PAPERBACK & KINDLE

Printed in Great Britain
by Amazon.co.uk, Ltd.,
Marston Gate.